VEGAN GOURMET
RECIPES FOR ENTERTAINING

VEGAN GOURMET
RECIPES FOR ENTERTAINING

90 imaginative recipes that are perfect for special occasions, from sumptuous soups and appetizers to main courses, sides and desserts, shown in 300 step-by-step photographs

TONY & YVONNE BISHOP-WESTON

southwater

This edition is published by Southwater, an imprint of Anness Publishing Ltd, Blaby Road, Wigston, Leicestershire LE18 4SE

Email: info@anness.com

Web: www.southwaterbooks.com; www.annesspublishing.com

If you like the images in this book and would like to investigate using them for publishing, promotions or advertising, please visit our website www.practicalpictures.com for more information.

Publisher: Joanna Lorenz
Editors: Elizabeth Woodland and Kate Eddison
Copy Editor: Jay Thundercliffe
Design: Nigel Partridge
Production Controller: Christine Ni

Main front cover image shows Sweet Pumpkin and Peanut Curry – for recipe, see page 48

Previously published as part of a larger volume, *The Complete Book of Vegan Cooking*

NOTES

• Bracketed terms are intended for American readers.
• For all recipes, quantities are given in both metric and imperial measures and, where appropriate, in standard cups and spoons.
• Follow one set of measures, but not a mixture, because they are not interchangeable.
• Standard spoon and cup measures are level. 1 tsp = 5ml, 1 tbsp = 15ml, 1 cup = 250ml/8fl oz.
• Australian standard tablespoons are 20ml.
• Australian readers should use 3 tsp in place of 1 tbsp for measuring small quantities.
• American pints are 16fl oz/2 cups. American readers should use 20fl oz/ 2.5 cups in place of 1 pint when measuring liquids.
• Electric oven temperatures in this book are for conventional ovens. When using a fan oven, the temperature will probably need to be reduced by about 10–20ºC/ 20–40ºF. Since ovens vary, you should check with your manufacturer's instruction book for guidance.
• The nutritional analysis given for each recipe is calculated per portion (i.e. serving or item), unless otherwise stated.
• If the recipe gives a range, such as Serves 4–6, then the nutritional analysis will be for the smaller portion size, i.e. 6 servings.
• Measurements for sodium do not include salt added to taste.
• Medium (US large) eggs are used unless otherwise stated.

ETHICAL TRADING POLICY
At Anness Publishing we believe that business should be conducted in an ethical and ecologically sustainable way, with respect for the environment and a proper regard to the replacement of the natural resources we employ.

As a publisher, we use a lot of wood pulp to make high-quality paper for printing, and that wood commonly comes from spruce trees. We are therefore currently growing more than 750,000 trees in three Scottish forest plantations: Berrymoss (130 hectares/320 acres), West Touxhill (125 hectares/305 acres) and Deveron Forest (75 hectares/185 acres). The forests we manage contain more than 3.5 times the number of trees employed each year in making paper for the books we manufacture.

Because of this ongoing ecological investment programme, you, as our customer, can have the pleasure and reassurance of knowing that a tree is being cultivated on your behalf to naturally replace the materials used to make the book you are holding.

Our forestry programme is run in accordance with the UK Woodland Assurance Scheme (UKWAS) and will be certified by the internationally recognized Forest Stewardship Council (FSC). The FSC is a non-government organization dedicated to promoting responsible management of the world's forests. Certification ensures forests are managed in an environmentally sustainable and socially responsible way. For further information about this scheme, go to www.annesspublishing.com/trees

Contents

Introduction

Veganism is much more than simply a particular diet to be followed. There is a wide and varied philosophy and lifestyle behind it that incorporates many of the issues which are becoming growing concerns in the modern world, including animal welfare and environmental issues. The vegan lifestyle demands an awareness of much more than just the foods that are eaten. It can affect how and where you buy your food, the clothes you wear, the household products you use, and many more things.

People are now increasingly looking for a way of life to counteract many of the global issues and problems that face us. One of the most appropriate of those lifestyles is veganism.

Becoming a vegan is an important and potentially difficult decision to make, but once that choice is made, the vegan is faced with many hurdles when it comes to everyday life. Throwing a dinner party can be one of these daunting and confusing events. This book enables you to choose three delectable courses that will tempt your guests and demonstrate and celebrate the variety of foods that are available to vegans.

Below: There is no shortage of nutritious ingredients for vegans to use when cooking sumptuous dishes.

What is veganism?

In basic terms a vegan is someone who avoids consuming or utilizing any product that is, or was once, part of an animal or is sourced from an animal.

Humans are one of the most complex and adaptable species on the planet and can survive in many extremes and on a vast range of diets. Vegans believe that a varied plant-based diet produces the optimal state of physical and mental being, and that the principles of veganism are kinder to people, animals and the environment.

The Vegan Society, the first-ever vegan organization, which was founded in the UK in 1944, defines a vegan as a

Above: Vegans believe that a varied plant-based diet is the key to physical and mental wellbeing.

person who, "excludes all forms of exploitation of, and cruelty to, animals for food, clothing or any other purpose". The definitions of veganism in the many other vegan organizations around the world are fundamentally similar to this. Therefore, vegans seek to lead a lifestyle that is completely free from animal products for the benefit of all people, animals and the environment.

THE VEGAN SOCIETY DEFINITION OF VEGANISM

"The word 'veganism' denotes a philosophy and way of living which seeks to exclude – as far as is possible and practical – all forms of exploitation of, and cruelty to, animals for food, clothing or any other purpose; and by extension, promotes the development and use of animal-free alternatives for the benefit of humans, animals and the environment. In dietary terms it denotes the practice of dispensing with all products derived wholly or partly from animals."

Fundamentally, it is the risk of the exploitation and harm of a living creature and causing it suffering that is an important part of veganism – not just avoiding the direct responsibility of causing an animal's death, as is the case with vegetarianism.

Vegetarians may use and consume products that committed vegans avoid, because the products are made without actually killing an animal. Dairy products, such as milk and cheese, other animal-derived foods, such as honey, and materials derived in some way from animals, such as wool and silk, are available to the vegetarian because the animals are not killed in the process. Vegans, on the other hand, will avoid such products due to the exploitation and harm done to the animals merely by farming them for our benefit. Vegans use plant-based alternatives to milk, cheese and eggs, such as soya, and agave or maple syrup instead of honey. Vegans also use cotton, linen, hemp and synthetic fibres instead of silk, leather, wool and other items that are made from animals.

The minute details of how a product is made will have a big impact on whether it is acceptable to vegans. For example, beers and wines are often made with isinglass (made from the bladder of a fish) or gelatine, so vegans choose filtered alternatives or products fined with betonite (a mineral) or seaweed extracts. Vegan wines and beers are now widely available thanks to an interest in natural produce and a growing trend to avoid unnecessary additives.

Products that have been tested on animals are also avoided by vegans because of the harm they cause. Vegans prefer to use cosmetics and toiletries that are tested on humans or cells in a dish rather than cause suffering to animals.

The father of veganism, Donald Watson, who founded the Vegan Society in 1944, was a conscientious objector who believed that humans would always struggle to be kinder to fellow human beings if they failed to show compassion to voiceless and

helpless animals. He argued that true civilization depended on accepting the responsibilities we have that come with our human advantages of choice.

Rather than constantly having to argue and make decisions about an acceptable level of animal cruelty or discomfort, Watson insisted that vegans should simply opt out of exploitation of another sentient being's life and use the many ethical, practical and sustainable alternatives that nature provides us with.

Using this book
The biggest hurdle that many people have to overcome when following a vegan diet is not what to cook when

Left: Use alternatives to dairy and meat products, such as soya milk and yogurt, tofu and tempeh in your classic dishes.

they are preparing simple midweek meals for themselves and their families, but how to develop elegant recipes that can be served at vegan-friendly dinner parties, as well as for special-occcasion suppers. It is necessary for vegans, like everyone, to have plenty of exciting, healthy and delicious recipes up their sleeves that will impress dinner-party guests time and time again.

The following chapters will help to give you plenty of ideas for how to cook tasty and innovative vegan food for your friends and family. It is brimming with recipes that demonstrate the plethora of options that are available to vegans. These range from traditional entertaining fare that has been altered to make it vegan friendly, to really exciting new vegan dishes made from a medley of unusual and delicious ingredients.

The recipes in this book are split into convenient chapters to help you find the perfect dish for your dinner party, including Soups, Appetizers and Breads; Main Courses; Salads and Side Dishes; and Desserts, so it is simple to plan a mouthwatering menu for your guests.

Below: Vibrant, fresh and healthy, salads can be served as simple side dishes.

Planning a vegan menu

Preparing food for entertaining friends can be a little daunting at first but it is really no different than for anybody else, and may in fact be easier – you will not have to supply different food for meat-eaters and vegetarians, for one thing. It can also be more relaxing to be at a party where you have created the menu, and it is a great opportunity to show off all the delicious dishes that vegans eat.

There are few things in life more pleasant than sharing good food with friends. When hosting a dinner party, the main trick is to serve the food you love and let your guests share your passion.

There are many factors to take into consideration when preparing for your dinner party, such as what ingredients to buy, where to buy them, and where they should be sourced from, as well as what drinks to buy and serve with your meal.

Shopping for ingredients

Far from being limited to the food products you consume, veganism encompasses decisions you make for all your purchases, from the clothes on your back to the shoes on your feet and the cleaning products you use. Here, however, we will concentrate on shopping for food and drink.

Below: Join a box scheme run by a local farm to get fresh, seasonal produce without the packaging.

Your local supermarkets may seem difficult to navigate when you are concerning yourself with the origin of your food, as products are not always labelled clearly.

Look for organic produce, which has increased in popularity in the last ten years as consumers recognize the environmental damage caused by some methods used in conventional farming, as well as the nutritional value of organic produce. Stock-free farming, or vegan-organic growing, is similar. It avoids all artificial chemical products (synthetic fertilizer, pesticides, growth regulators), genetically modified organisms, animal manures and slaughterhouse by-products (blood, fish meal, bone meal, etc).

You can also look out for fairtrade products, where the organization tries to bring producers closer to their market, cutting out the middle-men, so that they get a bigger share of the price of the final product. Co-ops, too, are an ethical source of food. These are customer- or producer-owned schemes where all profits are shared out or ploughed back into the business to allow more ethical practices and decisions unmotivated by profit. Many label products such as wine and beer with the true ingredients, including production aids, such as gelatine. They are an excellent example of a retailer labelling vegan products.

Above: Buy your fruit and vegetables directly from the grower at local farmers' markets.

Outside of supermarkets, you could look at farmers' markets and vegetable box schemes. Farmers' markets are public markets where farmers and other vendors can sell their products directly to the consumer. It is another way of buying fresh, seasonal produce directly from the grower, and many of the farmers will be using organic methods. Vegetable box schemes also support organic, local farming. Consumers order seasonal produce directly from the local farmers and this is delivered to their homes or picked up, often just hours after harvesting. These schemes support the local economy; cut out some of the excessive profits that are made by supermarkets; reduce transportation of food and decrease unnecessary packaging. In the USA, community supported agriculture, or CSAs, are systems of buying local produce, similar to the box scheme. The system may vary but the arrangement is usually based on the farmer offering 'shares' in their crops. After harvesting, the subscribers or shareholders receive fresh produce.

The local health-food store is a great resource for buying vegan products that supermarkets do not think viable. They are also a good source of advice, as well as support in obtaining an item even if it is not already stocked.

Right: Often the simplest dishes are the most delicious. This Pea Soup with Garlic will be a great crowd pleaser.

If you cannot find what you are looking for, then the internet is an excellent resource. There are dedicated on-line retailers selling all the vegan products you could imagine. Up-to-date lists of products are also published by a number of organizations. In the UK, the *Animal Free Shopper* is an excellent resource and is published every couple of years by The Vegan Society. For vegans in the USA, PETA publish a cruelty-free shopping guide to help consumers find products that are not tested on animals. Vegetarian and vegan magazines also have a useful classified section in the back.

Preparing for special meals

Ensure that you are aware of any allergies your guests may have before planning your menu. Many vegans find themselves catering for dedicated meat-eaters, which can be an enjoyable experience because you get a chance to show them the array of colours, flavours and tastes of well-produced vegan cuisine. If you are aiming for a classy dinner party then spend accordingly on your meal. Look to include a few exotic ingredients in the dishes, and present your food with plenty of style.

The trick to a successful dinner party is to have as much as possible prepared ahead so you actually get to spend time with your guests rather than being stuck in the kitchen. Perhaps serve soup or a cold appetizer, then something that just needs taking out of the oven and heating up gently while you eat your first course.

What to serve will be, to some extent, influenced by the time of year, as well as the occasion. For an informal gathering of friends in winter, what could be nicer than a warming hotpot that has been cooking for a long time, such as Black Bean Hotpot. For an elegant summer dinner party, try serving something that looks unusual, such as Pumpkin stuffed with Pistachio, Saffron and Apricot Pilaff.

The presentation will be much more impressive if you make individual portions of items such as pies or tarts. Other dishes, such as rice or stir-fries, can be presented in a large hollowed out tomato, half a green (bell) pepper, a large flat mushroom or a potato skin. You can easily make filo baskets by draping the pastry over an oiled ramekin and then baking it before filling with your food.

Informal gatherings are good for a big pan of food from which people can help themselves. Pots full of casseroles, stews and curries are ideal for this situation and often you can simply have a side serving of rice, couscous or bread to go along with the main dish.

You can also top pots of stew or curry with pastry or potato scallops or mashed sweet potato sprinkled with seeds, if you like.

For dessert, try pre-prepared scoops of vegan ice cream covered in melted chocolate and served with hot whisky or orange liqueur. If you feel confident you can even create a flaming dessert – very impressive in a romantically lit room. Other options include creating a sorbet using fresh fruit, such as pears or clementines, and then packing the sorbet in the hollowed-out fruit. There is no rule that says you have to prepare everything yourself, so why not treat your guests to a store-bought vegan dessert, if your time is limited.

Below: Artichokes with Beans and Almonds will make an ideal dish for a sophisticated dinner party.

Below: Curried Leek and Squash Gratin is perfect for serving a group of hungry friends at an informal gathering.

soups, appetizers and breads

The first course of your dinner party is important as it whets the appetite and gives your guests a feel for what is to come. Whether you want a warming soup or a delicate appetizer, this chapter is full of delicious ideas. Roasted Root Vegetable Soup or Red Bean Soup with Salsa are ideal as they are so tasty and nutritious. Hummus or Aubergine Dip make a great snack with homemade bread, or for a special occasion you can impress guests with tofu Dragon Balls or Spicy Pea Pakora.

Pea soup with garlic

This fresh-tasting soup is simple and quick to prepare. It has a wonderfully sweet flavour and smooth texture, and is great served with crusty bread and garnished with mint.

Serves 4

30ml/2 tbsp olive oil
1 garlic clove, crushed
900g/2lb/8 cups frozen peas
1.2 litres/2 pints/5 cups vegetable stock
25g/1oz/2 tbsp soya margarine
salt and ground black pepper

1 Heat the olive oil in a large pan and add the garlic. Fry gently for about 2–3 minutes, until softened, then add the peas. Cook for 1–2 minutes more, then pour in the stock.

Cook's tip
If you keep a bag of frozen peas in the freezer, you can rustle up this soup at very short notice.

2 Bring the soup to the boil, then reduce the heat to a simmer. Cover and cook for 5–6 minutes, until the peas are tender. Leave to cool slightly, then transfer the mixture to a food processor and process until smooth (you may have to do this in two batches).

3 Return the soup to the pan and heat through gently. Season with salt and pepper to taste and stir in the soya margarine.

Energy 283kcal/1167kJ; Protein 15.5g; Carbohydrate 25.5g, of which sugars 5.2g; Fat 14g, of which saturates 3.7g; Cholesterol 1mg; Calcium 48mg; Fibre 10.6g; Sodium 52mg.

Pumpkin soup with cinnamon

Colourful pumpkin is full of flavour, making it ideal for this delicious winter soup. Garnish with rice and serve with crusty bread for a substantial and warming meal.

Serves 4

1.1kg/2lb 7oz pumpkin
750ml/1¼ pints/3 cups vegetable stock
750ml/1¼ pints/3 cups soya milk
10–15ml/2–3 tsp agave syrup
75g/3oz/½ cup cooked rice
5ml/1 tsp ground cinnamon
30ml/2 tbsp pumpkin oil
salt and ground black pepper

Variation
This soup is also delicious if made with butternut squash in place of the pumpkin.

1 Cut the pumpkin into wedges. Remove the seeds, cut off the peel and chop the flesh into chunks.

2 Place the pumpkin in a pan and add the stock, milk and syrup, and season with salt and black pepper.

3 Bring the mixture gently to the boil, then reduce the heat and simmer for about 15–20 minutes, or until the pumpkin is tender.

4 Drain the pumpkin, reserving the cooking liquid, and purée it in a food processor or blender, then return it to the pan with the liquid and add the ground cinnamon.

5 Bring the soup back to the boil for a minute. Check the seasoning and pour into warmed bowls. Garnish with some cooked rice, a sprinkling of ground cinnamon and a drizzle of pumpkin oil. Serve immediately.

Energy 182kcal/759kJ; Protein 8.1g; Carbohydrate 15.8g, of which sugars 8.2g; Fat 9.5g, of which saturates 1.7g; Cholesterol 0mg; Calcium 111mg; Fibre 2.8g; Sodium 67mg.

Potato and dulse soup

Dulse seaweed, with its uniquely tangy taste, is an excellent ingredient for vegans. It is a good source of minerals and vitamins and has a high protein content.

Serves 6–8

50g/2oz/¼ cup soya margarine
2 large onions, peeled and finely chopped
30ml/2 tbsp dried dulse seaweed
675g/1½lb potatoes, diced
about 1.75 litres/3 pints/7½ cups hot
  vegetable stock
a little soya milk, if necessary
sea salt and ground black pepper
chopped fresh chives, to garnish

1 Melt the soya margarine in a large heavy pan and add the onions, turning them until well coated. Cover and leave to sweat over a very low heat for about 10 minutes.

2 Add the seaweed and potatoes to the pan, and mix well. Season with salt and pepper, cover and cook without colouring over a gentle heat for about 10 minutes. Add the stock, bring to the boil and simmer for 25 minutes, or until the vegetables are tender.

3 Remove from the heat and allow to cool slightly. Purée the soup in batches in a blender or food processor.

4 Reheat the soup over a low heat and adjust the seasoning. If the soup seems too thick, add a little stock or milk.

5 Serve the soup very hot, sprinkled with chopped chives.

Cook's tip
For the best results use floury potatoes in this dish, such as Golden Wonder.

Energy 125kcal/523kJ; Protein 2.1g; Carbohydrate 17.7g, of which sugars 4g; Fat 5.6g, of which saturates 2.3g; Cholesterol 1mg; Calcium 18mg; Fibre 1.6g; Sodium 166mg.

Spanish almond and onion soup

The combination of onions, sherry and saffron gives this pale yellow soup a beguiling and distinctive flavour. It will make the perfect appetizer to a special vegan meal for friends or family.

Serves 4

45ml/3 tbsp coconut oil
2 large yellow onions, thinly sliced
1 small garlic clove, finely chopped
pinch of saffron threads
50g/2oz blanched almonds,
   toasted and finely ground
750ml/1¼ pints/3 cups vegetable stock
45ml/3 tbsp sherry
2.5ml/½ tsp paprika
salt and ground black pepper

To garnish
30ml/2 tbsp flaked (sliced) almonds, toasted
chopped fresh parsley

1 Heat the coconut oil in a heavy pan over a low heat. Add the onions and garlic, stirring to ensure that they are thoroughly coated in the oil.

2 Cover the pan and cook very gently, stirring frequently, for about 20 minutes, or until the onions have softened and turned golden yellow.

3 Add the saffron threads to the pan and cook, uncovered, for 3–4 minutes, then add the finely ground almonds and cook, stirring the ingredients constantly, for a further 2–3 minutes.

4 Pour the vegetable stock and sherry into the pan and stir in 5ml/1 tsp salt and the paprika. Season with plenty of black pepper. Bring to the boil, then lower the heat and simmer gently for about 10 minutes.

5 Pour the soup into a food processor or blender and process until smooth, then return it to the rinsed pan. Reheat slowly, without allowing the soup to boil, stirring occasionally. Taste for seasoning, adding more salt and pepper if required.

6 Ladle the soup into warmed bowls. Garnish each serving with the toasted flaked almonds and a little chopped fresh parsley and serve immediately.

Variation
This soup is also delicious served chilled. Add a little more vegetable stock to the soup to make it slightly thinner. Leave it to cool completely after cooking before chilling in the refrigerator for at least 4 hours. Just before serving, taste the soup for seasoning, and garnish as specified above.

Energy 255kcal/1054kJ; Protein 5.8g; Carbohydrate 11.5g, of which sugars 8.1g; Fat 19.6g, of which saturates 6.1g; Cholesterol 21mg; Calcium 82mg; Fibre 3.2g; Sodium 68mg.

Roasted root vegetable soup

Roasting the vegetables gives this winter soup a wonderful depth of flavour. You can use other vegetables, if you wish, or adapt the quantities depending on what is in season.

Serves 6

50ml/2fl oz/¼ cup olive oil
1 small butternut squash, peeled, seeded and cubed
2 carrots, cut into thick rounds
1 large parsnip, cubed
1 small swede (rutabaga), cubed
2 leeks, thickly sliced
1 onion, quartered
3 bay leaves
4 thyme sprigs, plus extra to garnish
3 rosemary sprigs
1.2 litres/2 pints/5 cups vegetable stock
salt and ground black pepper
soya yogurt, to garnish

1 Preheat the oven to 200°C/400°F/ Gas 6. Pour the olive oil into a large mixing bowl.

2 Add the prepared vegetables to the bowl and toss thoroughly with a spoon until they are all coated in the oil.

3 Spread out the vegetables in a single layer on one large or two small baking sheets. Tuck the bay leaves and the thyme and rosemary sprigs among the vegetables.

4 Roast the vegetables for 50 minutes or until tender, turning them occasionally to make sure they brown evenly.

5 Remove from the oven, discard the herbs and transfer the vegetables to a large pan.

6 Pour the stock into the pan and bring slowly to the boil. Reduce the heat, season to taste, then simmer gently for about 10 minutes.

7 Transfer the soup to a food processor or blender, or use a hand blender if you prefer, and process for a few minutes until thick and smooth.

8 Return the soup to the pan and heat it through for a minute or two. Season with salt and pepper and add a swirl of soya yogurt. Garnish each bowl with a sprig of thyme.

Energy 113kcal/473kJ; Protein 2.5g; Carbohydrate 12.4g, of which sugars 5.1g; Fat 6.3g, of which saturates 1g; Cholesterol 0mg; Calcium 50mg; Fibre 3.5g; Sodium 11mg.

Red bean soup with salsa

This mildly spiced soup is perfect for lunch on a lovely summer's day. A delicious cooling salsa of avocado and lime is added as a garnish for a special finishing touch.

Serves 6

30ml/2 tbsp olive oil
2 onions, chopped
2 garlic cloves, chopped
10ml/2 tsp ground cumin
1.5ml/¼ tsp cayenne pepper
15ml/1 tbsp paprika
15ml/1 tbsp tomato purée (paste)
2.5ml/½ tsp dried oregano
400g/14oz can chopped tomatoes
2 x 400g/14oz cans red kidney beans,
   drained and rinsed
900ml/1½ pints/3¾ cups vegetable stock
salt and ground black pepper
Tabasco sauce, to serve

For the guacamole salsa
2 avocados
1 small red onion, finely chopped
1 green chilli, seeded and finely chopped
15ml/1 tbsp chopped fresh coriander (cilantro)
juice of 1 lime

1 Heat the oil in a large, heavy pan and add the onions and garlic. Cook for about 4–5 minutes, until softened. Add the cumin, cayenne and paprika, and cook for 1 minute, stirring continuously.

2 Stir the tomato purée into the pan and cook for a few seconds, then stir in the oregano. Add the chopped tomatoes and kidney beans, and then pour in the vegetable stock.

3 Bring the tomato and bean mixture to the boil and simmer for 15–20 minutes. Cool the soup slightly, then purée it in a food processor or blender until smooth. Return to the rinsed-out pan and add seasoning to taste.

4 To make the guacamole salsa, halve, stone (pit) and peel the avocados, then dice them finely. Place in a small bowl and gently, but thoroughly, mix with the finely chopped red onion and chilli, and the coriander and lime juice.

5 Reheat the soup and ladle into bowls. Spoon a little guacamole salsa into the middle of each and serve, offering Tabasco sauce for those who want to spice up their soup.

Cook's tip
This is the perfect soup to make in a big batch and freeze in small portions ready to thaw.

Energy 302kcal/1265kJ; Protein 11.7g; Carbohydrate 33.2g, of which sugars 11.8g; Fat 14.5g, of which saturates 2.8g; Cholesterol 0mg; Calcium 125mg; Fibre 11.8g; Sodium 537mg.

Leek and vegetable soup with sun-dried tomato bread

Thickening this dish with a little oatmeal provides extra protein and fibre to this tasty and nourishing soup. The tangy tomato bread makes the perfect accompaniment.

Serves 4

2 small parsnips, quartered lengthways
4 red onions, cut into thin wedges
4 carrots, thickly sliced
4 leeks, thickly sliced
1 small swede (rutabaga), cut into chunks
4 medium potatoes, cut into chunks
30ml/2 tbsp olive oil
few sprigs of fresh thyme, plus a few extra
    sprigs to garnish
1 bulb garlic, broken into cloves, unpeeled
1 litre/1¾ pints/4 cups vegetable stock
90ml/6 tbsp rolled oats
salt and ground black pepper

For the sun-dried tomato bread
1 ciabatta loaf (about 275g/10oz)
60ml/4 tbsp olive oil
1 garlic clove, crushed
4 sun-dried tomatoes, finely chopped
30ml/2 tbsp chopped fresh parsley

1 Preheat the oven to 200°C/400°F/ Gas 6. Cut the thick ends of the parsnip quarters into four, then place them in a large roasting pan. Add the onions, carrots, leeks, swede and potatoes, and spread them in an even layer.

2 Drizzle the olive oil over the vegetables. Add the thyme and unpeeled garlic cloves. Toss well and roast for 45 minutes, until all the vegetables are tender and well browned in places.

3 Meanwhile, to make the sun-dried tomato bread, cut diagonal slits along the loaf, taking care not to cut right through it. Mix the olive oil with the garlic, chopped sun-dried tomatoes and parsley.

4 Carefully spread the mixture into each slit in the loaf, then press the bread back together. Wrap the loaf in foil and bake in the hot oven for 15 minutes, opening the foil for the remaining 4–5 minutes so that the top of the loaf can crisp up slightly.

5 Discard the thyme from the roasted vegetables. Squeeze all the garlic cloves from their skins over the other vegetables in the pan.

6 Process about half the vegetables with the stock and oats in a food processor or blender until smooth.

7 Pour the pureé into a pan, bring to the boil and season to taste. Add the remaining vegetables and heat through.

8 Ladle the soup into bowls and garnish with fresh thyme sprigs. Serve the hot tomato bread with the soup.

Variation
Try using cooked pearl barley or wild rice in place of the oats.

Energy 684kcal/2878kJ; Protein 19.2g; Carbohydrate 104.6g, of which sugars 28.1g; Fat 23.9g, of which saturates 3.2g; Cholesterol 0mg; Calcium 288mg; Fibre 16.6g; Sodium 458mg.

Pearl barley and haricot bean soup with mushrooms

This hearty main meal vegetable soup is perfect on a freezing cold day. Serve in warmed bowls, with plenty of rye or pumpernickel bread on the side.

Serves 6

30ml/2 tbsp haricot (navy) beans, soaked overnight
2 litres/3½ pints/8 cups water or vegetable stock
45ml/3 tbsp green split peas
45ml/3 tbsp yellow split peas
90ml/6 tbsp pearl barley
1 onion, chopped
3 celery sticks, diced or sliced
5 garlic cloves, sliced
2 carrots, sliced
1 large baking potato, peeled and cut into chunks
10g/¼oz mixed dried mushrooms
ground black pepper
chopped fresh parsley, to garnish

1 Put the beans in a large pan, cover with water or vegetable stock and bring to the boil. Boil for 10 minutes, then skim any froth from the surface. Add the green and yellow split peas, pearl barley, onion, celery and garlic.

2 Bring the mixture to the boil, then reduce the heat, cover and simmer gently for about 1½ hours, or until the beans are tender.

Cook's tip
Dried beans should be soaked in a bowl of cold water overnight to reduce the cooking time.

3 Add the carrots, potato and dried mushrooms and cook for a further 30 minutes, or until the beans and vegetables are tender.

4 Season to taste, then ladle into bowls, garnish with parsley and serve with rye or pumpernickel bread.

Energy 162kcal/689kJ; Protein 6.8g; Carbohydrate 34.1g, of which sugars 4.3g; Fat 0.8g, of which saturates 0.1g; Cholesterol 0mg; Calcium 34mg; Fibre 2.9g; Sodium 30mg.

Japanese miso broth with tofu

This flavoursome broth is simple and highly nutritious. In Japan, it is traditionally eaten for breakfast, but it also makes a great appetizer or light lunch.

2 Heat the mixture over a low heat until boiling, then lower the heat and simmer for 10 minutes. Strain the broth, return it to the pan and reheat until simmering. Add the green sliced spring onions or leeks and the pak choi or Asian greens and tofu. Cook for 2 minutes.

3 In a small bowl, combine the miso with a little soup, then stir the mixture into the pan. Add soy sauce to taste.

4 Coarsely chop the coriander leaves and stir most of them into the soup with the white part of the spring onions or leeks. Cook for 1 minute.

5 Ladle the soup into warmed bowls. Sprinkle with the remaining chopped coriander and the shredded fresh red chilli, if using, and serve immediately.

Serves 4

1 bunch of spring onions (scallions) or
    5 baby leeks
15g/½oz fresh coriander (cilantro)
3 thin slices fresh root ginger
2 star anise
1 small dried red chilli
1.2 litres/2 pints/5 cups dashi or
    vegetable stock
225g/8oz pak choi (bok choy) or other Asian
    greens, thickly sliced
200g/7oz firm tofu, cut into 2.5cm/1in cubes
60ml/4 tbsp red miso
30–45ml/2–3 tbsp Japanese soy sauce
1 fresh red chilli, seeded and
    shredded (optional)

1 Cut the coarse green tops off the spring onions or baby leeks and slice the rest of the spring onions or leeks finely on the diagonal. Place the green tops in a large pan with the stalks from the coriander, the ginger, star anise, dried chilli and dashi or stock.

Cook's tip
Accompany with rice cakes, or for a more substantial snack, add noodles, simmered for the time suggested on the packet.

Energy 71kcal/297kJ; Protein 7.2g; Carbohydrate 4.2g, of which sugars 3.5g; Fat 2.9g, of which saturates 0.4g; Cholesterol 0mg; Calcium 372mg; Fibre 2.6g; Sodium 884mg.

Hummus

This classic Greek dip is flavoured with garlic and tahini – sesame seed paste. For a fuller flavour, add a little ground cumin or roasted red (bell) pepper. Serve with toasted pitta bread.

Serves 4–6

400g/14oz can chickpeas, drained
60ml/4 tbsp tahini
2–3 garlic cloves, crushed
60ml/4 tbsp rapeseed (canola) oil
juice of ½–1 lemon
salt and ground black pepper

Health benefit

Hummus makes a good filling for baked potatoes, lowering their overall GI value and adding protein, especially served with a mixed salad or followed by fresh fruit.

1 Set aside a few of the chickpeas to use as a garnish, then coarsely mash the rest in a mixing bowl using a potato masher. If you prefer a smoother purée, then process the chickpeas in a food processor or blender until they form a smooth paste.

2 Mix the tahini into the bowl of chickpeas, then stir in the crushed garlic cloves and rapeseed oil, and add lemon juice, to taste. Season with salt and black pepper and garnish the top with the reserved chickpeas. Serve the dip at room temperature.

Energy 140kcal/586kJ; Protein 6.9g; Carbohydrate 11.2g, of which sugars 0.4g; Fat 7.8g, of which saturates 1.1g; Cholesterol 0mg; Calcium 97mg; Fibre 3.6g; Sodium 149mg.

Aubergine dip

Known as baba ghanoush in the Middle East, this dip has a delicious taste and a soft, velvety texture. Eat with pitta bread, breadsticks or tortilla chips, or spread on slices of bread.

Serves 4–6

1 large aubergine (eggplant)
30ml/2 tbsp olive oil
1 small onion, finely chopped
2 garlic cloves, finely chopped
45ml/3 tbsp chopped fresh parsley
75ml/5 tbsp silken tofu
Tabasco sauce, to taste
juice of 1 lemon, to taste
salt and ground black pepper

Cook's tip

You can roast the aubergine in the oven at 200°C/400°F/Gas 6 for 20 minutes, if you prefer.

1 Preheat the grill (broiler). Place the whole aubergine on a baking sheet and place it under the hot grill for about 20–30 minutes, turning occasionally. Cook until the skin has turned black and become wrinkled, and the aubergine flesh feels soft and tender when pressed with a fork.

2 Cover the aubergine with a clean dish towel and then set it aside to cool for 5 minutes.

3 Heat the olive oil in a frying pan and cook the finely chopped onion and garlic for 5 minutes, or until softened but not browned.

4 Peel the skin from the aubergine. Mash the flesh into a pulpy purée.

5 Stir in the onion mixture, parsley and tofu. Add the Tabasco sauce, lemon juice and seasoning to taste.

6 Serve spread on toast or crusty bread or use as a dip with pitta bread or corn chips, if you prefer.

Energy 129kcal/535kJ; Protein 3.3g; Carbohydrate 1.9g, of which sugars 1.6g; Fat 12.2g, of which saturates 1.6g; Cholesterol 0mg; Calcium 85mg; Fibre 2.5g; Sodium 4mg.

Dolmades

For a tasty appetizer to start a vegan dinner party, try these vine leaves stuffed with spiced brown rice, nuts and fruit. The filling is infused with sumac, which has a sharp lemon flavour.

Serves 4–5

20 vacuum-packed vine leaves in brine
90g/3½oz/½ cup long grain brown rice
25ml/1½ tbsp olive oil
1 small onion, finely chopped
50g/2oz/½ cup pine nuts
45ml/3 tbsp raisins
30ml/2 tbsp chopped fresh mint
2.5ml/½ tsp ground cinnamon
2.5ml/½ tsp ground allspice
10ml/2 tsp ground sumac
10ml/2 tsp lemon juice
30ml/2 tbsp tomato purée (paste)
salt and ground black pepper
lemon slices and mint sprigs, to garnish

1 Rinse the vine leaves well under cold running water, then drain. Bring a pan of lightly salted water to the boil. Add the rice, lower the heat, cover and simmer for 10–12 minutes, or until almost cooked. Drain.

2 Heat 10ml/2 tsp of the olive oil in a non-stick frying pan, add the onion and cook until soft. Stir in the pine nuts and cook until lightly browned, then add the raisins, chopped mint, cinnamon, allspice and sumac, with salt and pepper to taste. Stir in the rice and mix well. Leave to cool.

Cook's tip
Vacuum-packed vine leaves are available from Middle Eastern food stores and good delicatessens.

3 Line a pan with any damaged vine leaves. Trim the stalks from the remaining leaves and lay them flat. Place a little filling on each. Fold the sides over and roll up each leaf neatly. Place the dolmades side by side in the leaf-lined pan, so that they fit tightly.

4 Mix 300ml/½ pint/1¼ cups water with the lemon juice and tomato purée in a small bowl. Whisk in the remaining olive oil until the mixture is well blended.

5 Pour the mixture over the dolmades in the pan and place a heatproof plate on top to keep them in place.

6 Cover the pan and simmer the dolmades for about 1 hour, or until all the liquid has been absorbed and the leaves are tender.

7 Transfer the dolmades to a platter, garnish with lemon slices and mint sprigs and serve hot or cold.

Energy 43kcal/181kJ; Protein 0.7g; Carbohydrate 6.7g, of which sugars 1.7g; Fat 1.1g, of which saturates 0.1g; Cholesterol 0mg; Calcium 12mg; Fibre 0.3g; Sodium 2mg.

Beansprout and cucumber parcels

This is inspired by a typical Vietnamese snack. These delightful rice paper rolls filled with crunchy raw summer vegetables and fresh mint and coriander are light and refreshing, either as a snack or an appetizer to a meal. A great gluten-free option for friends who cannot have wheat.

Serves 4

12 round rice papers
1 medium lettuce, leaves separated and
   ribs removed
2–3 carrots, cut into julienne strips
1 small cucumber, peeled, halved lengthways
   and seeded, and cut into julienne strips
3 spring onions (scallions), trimmed and cut
   into julienne strips
225g/8oz mung beansprouts
1 small bunch fresh mint leaves,
   roughly chopped
1 small bunch fresh coriander (cilantro)
   leaves, roughly chopped
dipping sauce, to serve

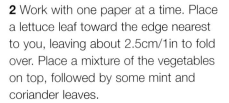

1 Pour some lukewarm water into a shallow dish. Soak the rice papers, two or three at a time, for 5 minutes until pliable. Place the soaked papers on a clean dish towel and cover with a second dish towel to keep them moist.

2 Work with one paper at a time. Place a lettuce leaf toward the edge nearest to you, leaving about 2.5cm/1in to fold over. Place a mixture of the vegetables on top, followed by some mint and coriander leaves.

3 Fold the edge nearest to you over the filling, tuck in the sides, and roll tightly to the edge on the far side. Place the filled roll on a plate and cover with clear film (plastic wrap), so it does not dry out. Repeat with the remaining rice papers and vegetables.

4 Serve the rolls with a dipping sauce of your choice. If you are making these summer rolls ahead of time, keep them in the refrigerator under a damp dish towel, so that they remain moist.

Cook's tip
Rice papers are readily available in Chinese and Asian markets.

Energy 105kcal/441kJ; Protein 4g; Carbohydrate 20g, of which sugars 6.6g; Fat 1g, of which saturates 0.2g; Cholesterol 0mg; Calcium 74mg; Fibre 3.7g; Sodium 23mg.

Courgette fritters

A healthier twist on Japanese tempura, using Indian spices and gram flour – made from chickpeas – in the batter. The result is a wonderful snack that has a light, crispy coating, while the courgette baton inside becomes meltingly tender.

Serves 4

90g/3½oz/¾ cup gram flour
5ml/1 tsp baking powder
2.5ml/½ tsp ground turmeric
10ml/2 tsp ground coriander
5ml/1 tsp ground cumin
5ml/1 tsp chilli powder
250ml/8fl oz/1 cup bottled beer
600g/1lb 6oz courgettes (zucchini), cut
   into batons
sunflower oil, for deep-frying
sea salt
steamed basmati rice, soya yogurt and
   pickles, to serve

1 Sift the gram flour, baking powder, turmeric, coriander, cumin and chilli powder into a large bowl. Stir lightly to mix through.

2 Season the mixture with salt and then gradually add the beer, mixing gently as you pour it in, to make a thick batter – be careful not to overmix.

3 Fill a large wok or deep, heavy pan one-third full with sunflower oil and heat to 180°C/350°F or until a cube of bread, dropped into the oil, browns in about 45 seconds.

4 Working in batches, dip the courgette batons in the batter and then deep-fry for 1–2 minutes until crisp and golden. Lift out of the wok using a slotted spoon. Drain on kitchen paper and keep warm.

5 Serve immediately with steamed basmati rice, soya yogurt and pickles.

Energy 207kcal/857kJ; Protein 8.3g; Carbohydrate 10.8g, of which sugars 4.7g; Fat 14.8g, of which saturates 2.4g; Cholesterol 95mg; Calcium 104mg; Fibre 2.1g; Sodium 50mg.

Crispy onion fritters

These delicious Indian snacks are made with gram flour, otherwise known as chickpea flour or besan, which has a distinctive nutty flavour. Serve with chutney or a soya yogurt and mint dip.

3 Add the gram flour and baking powder to the onion mixture in the bowl, then use your hand to mix all the ingredients thoroughly.

4 Shape the mixture by hand into approximately 12–15 fritters, about the size of golf balls.

5 Heat the rapeseed oil for deep-frying to 180–190°C/350–375°F, or until a cube of day-old bread browns in about 45 seconds. Fry the fritters in batches until golden brown all over. Remove with a slotted spoon, drain on kitchen paper and keep warm while the rest are frying.

6 Serve the fritters warm accompanied by lemon wedges and a herby dip.

Serves 3–5

675g/1½lb onions, halved and thinly sliced
5ml/1 tsp sea salt
5ml/1 tsp ground coriander
5ml/1 tsp ground cumin
2.5ml/½ tsp ground turmeric
1–2 green chillies, seeded and
 finely chopped
45ml/3 tbsp chopped fresh coriander (cilantro)
90g/3½oz/¾ cup gram flour
2.5ml/½ tsp baking powder
rapeseed (canola) oil, for deep-frying

To serve
lemon wedges (optional)
fresh coriander (cilantro) sprigs
soya yogurt and herb dip (see Cook's tip)

1 Place the onions in a colander, add the salt and toss. Place on a plate and leave to stand for 45 minutes, tossing once or twice. Rinse the onions, then squeeze out any excess moisture.

2 Place the onions in a bowl. Add the ground coriander, cumin, turmeric, finely chopped chillies and chopped fresh coriander. Mix well.

Cook's tip
To make a herb dip, stir 30ml/ 2 tbsp each of chopped fresh coriander (cilantro) and mint into about 225g/8oz/1 cup soya yogurt.

Energy 245kcal/1016kJ; Protein 3.5g; Carbohydrate 26.4g, of which sugars 7.8g; Fat 14.1g, of which saturates 1.4g; Cholesterol 0mg; Calcium 64mg; Fibre 2.8g; Sodium 402mg.

Spicy pea pakora

These pakora make a delicious bitesize snack packed full of pulses, vegetables and spices.
For an extra healthy meal, try serving them in a wholemeal pitta bread with salad for lunch.

Serves 4–6

250g/9oz/generous 1 cup yellow split peas
   or red lentils, soaked overnight
3–5 garlic cloves, chopped
30ml/2 tbsp roughly chopped fresh
   root ginger
120ml/4fl oz/½ cup chopped fresh coriander
   (cilantro) leaves
2.5–5ml/½–1 tsp ground cumin
1.5–2.5ml/¼–½ tsp ground turmeric
large pinch of cayenne pepper or ½–1 fresh
   green chilli, chopped
120ml/4fl oz/½ cup gram flour
5ml/1 tsp baking powder
30ml/2 tbsp couscous
2 large or 3 small onions, chopped
vegetable oil, for frying
salt and ground black pepper
lemon wedges, to serve

2 Add the cumin, turmeric, cayenne or fresh chilli, 2.5ml/½ tsp salt, 2.5ml/½ tsp pepper, the gram flour, baking powder and couscous to the mixture and combine. The mixture should form a thick batter. If it seems too thick, add a spoonful of soaking water and if it is too watery, add a little more flour or couscous. Mix in the onions.

3 Heat the oil in a wide, deep frying pan, to a depth of about 5cm/2in, until it is hot enough to brown a cube of bread in 45 seconds. Using two spoons, form the mixture into small balls, about the size of a walnut, and slip each one gently into the hot oil. Cook until golden brown on the underside, then turn and cook the second side until golden brown.

4 Remove from the hot oil with a slotted spoon and drain on kitchen paper. Transfer to a baking sheet and keep warm in the oven.

5 Serve the pakora hot or leave to cool and serve at room temperature with lemon wedges.

1 Drain the split peas or lentils, reserving a little of the soaking water. Put the chopped garlic and ginger in a food processor or blender and process until finely chopped. Add the drained peas or lentils, 15–30ml/1–2 tbsp of the reserved soaking water and the chopped coriander, and process the mixture to form a purée.

Variation
Finely chopped green beans or roughly mashed green peas can be added to the final pakora mix. They will add some extra colour and increase the nutritional value.

Energy 355kcal/1487kJ; Protein 13.5g; Carbohydrate 49.2g, of which sugars 5.3g; Fat 12.2g, of which saturates 1.2g; Cholesterol 0mg; Calcium 85mg; Fibre 4.7g; Sodium 25mg.

Pea and potato baked samosas

Most samosas are deep-fried but these healthier versions are baked in the oven. They are perfect for parties, since the pastries need no last-minute attention.

Makes 25

1 large potato, about 250g/9oz, diced
15ml/1 tbsp groundnut (peanut) oil
2 shallots, finely chopped
1 garlic clove, finely chopped
60ml/4 tbsp coconut milk
5ml/1 tsp hot curry paste
75g/3oz/¾ cup peas
juice of ½ lime
25 samosa wrappers or 10 x 5cm/4 x 2in
   strips of filo pastry
oil, for brushing
salt and ground black pepper

1 Preheat the oven to 220°C/425°F/ Gas 7. Bring a small pan of water to the boil, add the diced potato, cover and cook for 10–15 minutes, until tender. Drain and set aside.

2 Meanwhile, heat the groundnut oil in a wok or large frying pan. Add the shallots and cook over a medium heat, stirring occasionally, for 3–4 minutes.

3 Add the chopped garlic to the wok and cook for a further 2–3 minutes until the shallots are soft and golden.

4 Add the drained diced potato, the coconut milk, curry paste, peas and lime juice to the wok.

5 Mash the mixture coarsely with a wooden spoon. Season to taste with salt and pepper and cook over a low heat for 2–3 minutes. Remove the pan from the heat and set aside until the mixture has cooled a little.

6 Lay a samosa wrapper or filo strip flat on the work surface. Brush with a little oil, then place a generous teaspoonful of the mixture in the middle of one end. Turn one corner diagonally over the filling to meet the long edge.

7 Continue folding over the filling, keeping the triangular shape as you work down the strip. Brush with a little more oil if necessary and place on a baking sheet. Prepare all the other samosas in the same way.

8 Bake the samosas for 15 minutes, or until the pastry is golden and crisp. Leave them to cool for a few minutes before serving.

Energy 42kcal/178kJ; Protein 1.2g; Carbohydrate 8.5g, of which sugars 0.6g; Fat 0.6g, of which saturates 0.1g; Cholesterol 0mg; Calcium 14mg; Fibre 0.5g; Sodium 4mg.

Dragon balls

Tofu is wonderfully healthy and versatile. It is delicious in this Japanese dish, known as hiryozu, meaning flying dragon's head. They make excellent appetizers, or can be served as party snacks.

Serves 4

2 x 285g/10¼oz packets firm tofu
20g/¾oz carrot, peeled
40g/1½oz green beans
30ml/2 tbsp buckwheat flour
30ml/2 tbsp sake
10ml/2 tsp mirin
5ml/1 tsp sea salt
10ml/2 tsp light miso
10ml/2 tsp agave syrup
sunflower oil, for deep-frying

For the lime sauce
45ml/3 tbsp light miso
juice of ½ lime
5ml/1 tsp rice vinegar or mirin

To garnish
300g/11oz mooli (daikon), peeled
2 dried red chillies, halved and seeded
4 chives, finely chopped

1 Drain the tofu and wrap in a dish towel or kitchen paper. Set a chopping board on top and leave for 2 hours, or until it loses most of its liquid.

2 Cut the mooli for the garnish into about 4cm/1½in thick slices. Make three to four small holes in each slice with a skewer or chopstick and fill with chilli pieces. Leave for 15 minutes, then grate the mooli and chilli finely.

3 To make the tofu balls, chop the carrot finely. Trim and cut the beans into 5mm/¼in lengths. Cook both vegetables for 1 minute in boiling water.

4 In a food processor, blend the tofu, buckwheat flour, sake, mirin, salt, light miso and agave syrup until smooth. Transfer to a bowl and mix in the carrot and beans.

5 Fill a wok or pan with oil 4cm/1½in deep, and heat to 185°C/365°F.

6 Soak a piece of kitchen paper with a little vegetable oil, and lightly moisten your hands with it. Scoop about 40ml/2½ tbsp of the mixture in one hand and shape into a ball between your hands.

7 Carefully slide the ball into the oil and deep-fry until crisp and golden brown. Drain on kitchen paper. Repeat with the remaining mixture.

8 Arrange the tofu balls on a plate and sprinkle with chives. Put 30ml/2 tbsp grated mooli in each of four bowls. Mix the lime sauce ingredients in a bowl. Serve the tofu balls with the sauce to be mixed with mooli by each guest.

Energy 250kcal/1038kJ; Protein 12.4g; Carbohydrate 10.4g, of which sugars 3.1g; Fat 17.1g, of which saturates 2g; Cholesterol 0mg; Calcium 722mg; Fibre 0.5g; Sodium 649mg.

Tofu and courgettes in tomato sauce

This Mediterranean-style dish can be eaten hot or cold, and improves given a day or two in the refrigerator. It is a delicious accompaniment to nut roast, or enjoy it on its own with crusty bread.

Serves 4

30ml/2 tbsp olive oil
2 garlic cloves, finely chopped
4 large courgettes (zucchini), thinly sliced on
   the diagonal
250g/9oz firm tofu, drained and cubed
1 lemon
sea salt and ground black pepper

For the tomato sauce
10ml/2 tsp balsamic vinegar
5ml/1 tsp agave syrup
300ml/½ pint/1¼ cups passata (bottled
   strained tomatoes)
small bunch of fresh mint or parsley, chopped

1 First, make the tomato sauce. Place the vinegar, agave syrup and passata in a small pan. Heat the mixture gently, stirring occasionally, until just beginning to bubble. Add the fresh mint or parsley and heat through.

2 Meanwhile, heat the olive oil in a large non-stick wok or frying pan until very hot, then add the garlic and stir-fry for 30 seconds, until golden. Add the courgette slices and stir-fry over a high heat for about 5–6 minutes, or until golden around the edges. Remove from the pan.

3 Add the tofu to the pan and brown for a few minutes. Turn gently, then brown again. Grate the rind from half the lemon and reserve for the garnish. Squeeze the lemon juice over the tofu.

4 Season to taste with salt and black pepper, then leave to sizzle until all the lemon juice has evaporated. Gently stir the courgettes into the tofu until well combined, then remove the wok or pan from the heat.

5 Transfer the courgettes and tofu to a warm serving dish and pour the tomato sauce over the top. Sprinkle with the grated lemon rind. Taste and season with more salt and pepper, if necessary. Serve immediately with crusty bread or as a side dish to a nut roast, if you like.

Energy 141kcal/585kJ; Protein 8.8g; Carbohydrate 6.8g, of which sugars 6.3g; Fat 8.9g, of which saturates 1.3g; Cholesterol 0mg; Calcium 389mg; Fibre 2.4g; Sodium 181mg.

Vegetable kebabs with a harissa dip

These skewered vegetables are first coated in a spicy oil and lemon juice marinade before grilling. Serve with a fiery harissa and soya yogurt dip for a flavoursome, healthy meal.

Serves 4

2 aubergines (eggplants), cut into chunks
8 button (white) mushrooms
2 courgettes (zucchini), cut into chunks
2–3 red or green (bell) peppers, seeded and
   cut into chunks
12–16 cherry tomatoes
4 small red onions, quartered
60ml/4 tbsp olive oil
juice of ½ lemon
1 garlic clove, crushed
5ml/1 tsp ground coriander
5ml/1 tsp ground cinnamon
10ml/2 tsp dark soy sauce
10ml/2 tsp agave syrup
sea salt

For the harissa and yogurt dip
450g/1lb/2 cups soya yogurt or coconut cream
30–60ml/2–4 tbsp harissa
small bunch of fresh coriander (cilantro),
   finely chopped
small bunch of mint, finely chopped
salt and ground black pepper

1 Preheat the grill (broiler) on the hottest setting. Put all the vegetables in a large bowl. Mix together the olive oil, lemon juice, garlic, ground coriander, cinnamon, dark soy sauce, agave syrup and sea salt and pour the mixture over the vegetables.

2 Using your hands, turn the vegetables gently in the marinade until they are well coated. Thread them on to metal skewers, alternating the vegetables.

3 Cook the kebabs under the grill, turning them occasionally, until the vegetables are nicely browned all over.

4 Meanwhile make the dip. Put the yogurt in a bowl and beat in the harissa, making it as fiery in taste as you like. Add most of the chopped coriander and mint, reserving a little to garnish, and season well with salt and ground black pepper.

5 Serve the skewers immediately with the dip, garnished with the reserved herbs. While the vegetables are still hot, slide them off the skewers and dip them into the yogurt and harissa dip before eating. Serve with a green salad, brown rice or quinoa if you like, or inside a tortilla wrap.

Cook's tip
Make sure you cut the vegetables into even chunks, so they will cook at the same time under the grill (broiler).

Energy 305kcal/1267kJ; Protein 9.9g; Carbohydrate 24.8g, of which sugars 22.6g; Fat 19.1g, of which saturates 6.6g; Cholesterol 16mg; Calcium 230mg; Fibre 5.2g; Sodium 181mg.

Seeded herby oatcakes

Adding thyme and sunflower seeds to these delicious oatcakes makes them especially good for dipping into a bowl of hummus – or try them spread with avocado and Marmite.

Makes 32

175g/6oz/1½ cups wholemeal
  (whole-wheat) flour
175g/6oz/1½ cups fine oatmeal
5ml/1 tsp salt
1.5ml/¼ tsp bicarbonate of soda
  (baking soda)
90ml/6 tbsp coconut oil
15ml/1 tbsp fresh thyme leaves, chopped
30ml/2 tbsp sunflower seeds
rolled oats, for sprinkling

1 Preheat the oven to 150°C/300°F/ Gas 2. Sprinkle two ungreased, non-stick baking sheets with rolled oats and set aside.

2 Put the flour, oatmeal, salt and bicarbonate of soda in a large bowl and rub in the coconut oil until the mixture resembles fine breadcrumbs. Stir in the thyme leaves.

3 Add just enough cold water (about 90–105ml/6–7 tbsp) to the dry ingredients and mix to form a stiff but not sticky dough.

4 Gently knead the dough on a lightly floured surface until it becomes smooth, then cut it roughly in half. Roll out one piece on a lightly floured surface to make a 23–25cm/9–10in round, about 1cm/½in in thickness.

5 Sprinkle the sunflower seeds over the dough and press them in with the rolling pin. Cut into triangles and arrange on one of the baking sheets. Repeat with the remaining dough. Bake for 45–60 minutes until crisp but not brown. Cool on wire racks.

Energy 63kcal/264kJ; Protein 1.6g; Carbohydrate 7.7g, of which sugars 0.1g; Fat 3.1g, of which saturates 1.8g; Cholesterol 0mg; Calcium 6mg; Fibre 0.9g; Sodium 2mg.

Rosemary focaccia

If you do not need both loaves, freeze one for another time and warm it in the oven before serving. Sprinkle the loaves with finely chopped garlic, if you prefer.

Makes 2 loaves

675g/1½lb/6 cups strong white
  bread flour
15ml/1 tbsp easy-blend (rapid-rise)
  dried yeast
75ml/5 tbsp olive oil
45ml/3 tbsp chopped fresh rosemary

Cook's tip
Put a bowl of water in the oven with the focaccia to prevent it from drying out too much as it bakes.

1 Put the flour and yeast in a large bowl with 5ml/1 tsp salt. Stir in 45ml/3 tbsp of the oil and 450ml/¾ pint/scant 2 cups lukewarm water. Mix with a round-bladed knife, then by hand to a soft dough, adding a little more lukewarm water if the dough feels dry.

2 Turn the dough out on to a lightly floured surface and knead for 10 minutes, until it is smooth and elastic. Put it in a lightly oiled bowl and cover with oiled clear film (plastic wrap). Leave in a warm place for about 1 hour, until the dough has doubled in size.

3 Preheat the oven to 200°C/400°F/ Gas 6. Turn out the dough on to a floured surface and cut it in half. Roll out each half into a 25cm/10in round. Transfer the rounds to greased baking sheets, cover with lightly oiled clear film and leave for 20 minutes, until risen.

4 Press your fingers into the dough to make deep holes all over it about 3cm/1¼ in apart. Leave for a further 5 minutes.

5 Sprinkle with the rosemary and plenty of sea salt. Sprinkle with water to keep the crust moist and bake for 25 minutes, until pale golden. Remove from the oven and drizzle with the remaining olive oil. Transfer to a wire rack to cool.

Energy 1436kcal/6068kJ; Protein 34.8g; Carbohydrate 266g, of which sugars 5.1g; Fat 33.1g, of which saturates 4.6g; Cholesterol 0mg; Calcium 575mg; Fibre 10.5g; Sodium 18mg.

Three seed loaf

Cornmeal and a cornucopia of seeds give this superb loaf a delicious flavour and unique texture. It is perfect served with a hummus dip.

3 Turn out the dough on to a lightly floured surface and knead for about 5 minutes until smooth and elastic.

4 Place in a lightly oiled bowl, cover with lightly oiled clear film (plastic wrap) and leave to rise, in a warm place, for about 1 hour, or until doubled in size.

5 Turn out the dough on to a lightly floured surface and knock back (punch down). Gently knead the pumpkin and sesame seeds into the dough. Shape into a round ball and flatten slightly.

6 Place on the prepared baking sheet, cover with lightly oiled clear film or slide into a large, lightly oiled plastic bag and leave to rise in a warm place again for 45 minutes, or until doubled in size.

7 Meanwhile, preheat the oven to 200°C/400°F/Gas 6. Brush the top of the loaf with water and sprinkle evenly with the sunflower seeds. Bake the loaf for 30–35 minutes, or until it is golden and sounds hollow when tapped on the base. Transfer the loaf to a wire rack to cool completely.

Makes 1 Loaf

275g/10oz/2½ cups unbleached
  white bread flour
50g/2oz/½ cup cornmeal
5ml/1 tsp salt
20g/¾oz fresh yeast
120ml/4fl oz/½ cup lukewarm water
120ml/4fl oz/½ cup soya milk
15ml/1 tbsp pumpkin seeds
15ml/1 tbsp sesame seeds
30ml/2 tbsp sunflower seeds

1 Lightly grease a baking sheet. Sift the flours and salt into a large bowl.

2 Cream the yeast with a little of the water in a jug (pitcher). Stir in the remainder of the water and the soya milk. Pour this into the centre of the flour and mix to a fairly soft dough.

Energy 1511kcal/6371kJ; Protein 45.7g; Carbohydrate 259.7g, of which sugars 5.9g; Fat 37.2g, of which saturates 4.2g; Cholesterol 0mg; Calcium 553mg; Fibre 13.5g; Sodium 2016mg.

Tandoori rotis

These unleavened rotis are one of the many delicious breads from India. They would normally be baked in a clay oven called a tandoor but are easily cooked in a traditional oven, as here.

Makes 6

350g/12oz/3 cups wholemeal
  (whole-wheat) flour
5ml/1 tsp salt
250ml/8fl oz/1 cup water
30–45ml/2–3 tbsp coconut oil for brushing

1 Sift the flour and salt into a large bowl. Add the water and mix to a soft dough. Knead the dough on a lightly floured surface for 3–4 minutes until smooth.

2 Place the dough in a lightly oiled bowl, cover with lightly oiled clear film (plastic wrap). Leave to rest for 1 hour.

3 Turn out on to a lightly floured surface. Divide the dough into six pieces and shape each into a ball. Press out into a larger round with your hand, cover with lightly oiled clear film and leave to rest for 10 minutes.

4 Meanwhile, preheat the oven to 230°C/450°F/Gas 8. Place three baking sheets in the oven to heat. Roll the rotis into 15cm/6in rounds, place two on each baking sheet and bake in the oven for about 8–10 minutes. Lightly brush each roti with oil and serve warm.

Cook's tips
• The rotis are ready when light brown bubbles appear on the surface and they puff up slightly.
• Add in extra spices such as cumin or cardamom, if you like.

Energy 244kcal/1030kJ; Protein 5.5g; Carbohydrate 45.3g, of which sugars 0.9g; Fat 5.8g, of which saturates 2.5g; Cholesterol 0mg; Calcium 82mg; Fibre 1.8g; Sodium 329mg.

main courses

This chapter features dishes that take advantage of the huge variety of grains, beans, vegetables, pasta and rice that are available to those on a vegan diet to create stunning main courses. These delicious dishes are full of mouthwatering flavours, and bring together influences from cuisines across the world to create really impressive meals for your dinner-party guests. From Black Bean Hotpot and Vegetable Moussaka with Tofu Topping, to Sweet Pumpkin and Peanut Curry and Couscous with Dried Fruit and Nuts, you will be spoilt for choice with the tempting range on offer.

Artichokes with beans and almonds

Globe artichokes are a variety of perennial thistle and have been a renowned epicurean delight for hundreds of years. Prized by the ancient Romans and grown in the garden of Henry VIII, they are still well deserving of a place in every vegan's kitchen. In this dish from Turkey, the tender bottoms are filled with fresh broad beans and flavoured with dill.

Serves 4

275g/10oz/2 cups shelled broad
  (fava) beans
4 large globe artichokes
120ml/4fl oz/½ cup olive oil
juice of 1 lemon
10ml/2 tsp sugar
75g/3oz/¾ cup blanched almonds
1 small bunch of fresh dill, chopped
2 tomatoes, skinned, seeded and diced
sea salt

2 Prepare the artichokes. Cut off the stalks and pull off all the leaves. Dig out the hairy choke from the middle using a teaspoon, then cut away any hard bits with a small sharp knife and trim into a neat cup shape. Rub the cup-shaped bases – called bottoms – with a mixture of lemon juice and salt to prevent them from discolouring.

1 Put the beans in a pan of water and bring to the boil. Lower the heat, then simmer for 10–15 minutes or until tender. Drain and refresh under cold running water, then peel off the skins.

3 Place the prepared artichokes in a large, heavy pan. Mix together the olive oil, lemon juice and 50ml/2fl oz/¼ cup water and pour the mixture over the artichokes.

4 Cover the pan with a tight-fitting lid and bring to a simmer. Cook the artichokes in the lemon juice and olive oil mixture gently for about 20 minutes.

5 Add the sugar, prepared broad beans and blanched almonds to the pan. Cover again with the lid and continue to simmer gently for a further 10 minutes, or until the artichokes are tender.

Cook's tips

• When buying almonds, you should pick fresh-looking ones in their skins. Put them in a bowl and cover with boiling water. Leave them to soak for a few hours until the skins start to loosen, then rub off the skins with your fingers. If you have time to leave them for as long as 24 hours, the nuts will soften, too.

• Fresh globe artichokes should be treated the same as a bunch of fresh flowers. As soon as you get them home, place them in a jug (pitcher) of water until you are ready to use them.

6 Toss half the chopped dill into the pan and season with sea salt. Mix all the ingredients together, then turn off the heat. Leave the artichokes to cool in the pan.

7 Lift the artichokes out of the pan and place them hollow-side up in a large serving dish. Mix the diced tomatoes with the beans and almonds in the pan.

8 Spoon the bean and vegetable mixture into the middle of the artichokes and all around them. Garnish with the remaining dill. Leave to cool to room temperature, then serve.

Energy 351kcal/1455kJ; Protein 8.2g; Carbohydrate 13.4g, of which sugars 8.3g; Fat 29.8g, of which saturates 3.6g; Cholesterol 0mg; Calcium 110mg; Fibre 5.5g; Sodium 29mg.

Lentils with mushrooms and anis

Rich in protein, iron, calcium and magnesium, lentils have been shown to be beneficial to the health of our hearts. Aniseed liqueur adds a delicious flavour to this nutritious dish.

Serves 4

30ml/2 tbsp olive oil
1 large onion, sliced
2 garlic cloves, finely chopped
250g/9oz/3 cups brown cap
   (cremini) mushrooms, sliced
150g/5oz/generous ½ cup brown
   or green lentils, soaked overnight
4 tomatoes, cut in eighths
1 bay leaf
175ml/6fl oz/¾ cup vegetable stock
25g/1oz/½ cup chopped fresh parsley
30ml/2 tbsp anis spirit or anisette
pinch of paprika
sea salt and ground black pepper

1 Heat the oil in a flameproof casserole. Add the onion and fry gently, with the garlic, until softened but not browned.

2 Add the sliced mushrooms and stir to combine with the onion and garlic. Continue cooking, stirring gently, for a couple of minutes.

3 Add the lentils, tomatoes, bay leaf and the stock. Simmer gently, covered, for 35 minutes until the lentils are soft, and the liquid has almost disappeared.

4 Stir in the parsley and anis. Season with salt, paprika and black pepper. Serve immediately in individual bowls.

Energy 216kcal/910kJ; Protein 12.4g; Carbohydrate 29.3g, of which sugars 9.6g; Fat 4.5g, of which saturates 0.7g; Cholesterol 0mg; Calcium 72mg; Fibre 6.9g; Sodium 26mg.

Curried leek and squash gratin

You can use virtually any kind of squash for this tasty gratin, which is perfect for a warming and hearty meal on a chilly day. Patty pans and acorn squash or pumpkins could all be used.

Serves 4–6

450g/1lb peeled and seeded squash,
   cut into 1cm/½in slices
60ml/4 tbsp olive oil
450g/1lb leeks, cut into thick, diagonal slices
675g/1½lb tomatoes, peeled and
   thickly sliced
2.5ml/½ tsp ground nutmeg
2.5ml/½ tsp ground toasted cumin seeds
300ml/½ pint/1¼ cups coconut mik
1 fresh red chilli, seeded and sliced
1 garlic clove, finely chopped
15ml/1 tbsp chopped fresh mint
30ml/2 tbsp chopped fresh parsley
60ml/4 tbsp rolled oats
salt and ground black pepper

1 Steam the squash over boiling salted water for 10 minutes.

2 Heat half the oil in a frying pan and cook the leeks gently for 5–6 minutes until lightly coloured. Try to keep the slices intact. Preheat the oven to 190°C/375°F/Gas 5.

3 Layer the squash, leeks and tomatoes in a 2 litre/3½ pint/8 cup gratin dish, arranging them in rows. Sprinkle with salt, pepper, nutmeg and cumin seeds.

Variation

For a curried version of this dish, use ground coriander as well as cumin. Use fresh coriander (cilantro) instead of the mint and parsley.

4 Pour the coconut milk into a small pan and add the sliced chilli, chopped garlic and mint. Bring to the boil over a low heat, then stir in the mint. Pour the mixture evenly over the layered vegetables, using a rubber spatula to scrape all the sauce out of the pan.

5 Cook for about 50–55 minutes, or until the gratin is bubbling and tinged brown. Sprinkle the parsley and oats on top and drizzle over the remaining oil. Bake for another 15–20 minutes until the oats have turned brown and crispy. Serve the gratin immediately.

Energy 248kcal/1032kJ; Protein 5.7g; Carbohydrate 16.7g, of which sugars 7.8g; Fat 18g, of which saturates 7.4g; Cholesterol 28mg; Calcium 126mg; Fibre 3.8g; Sodium 104mg.

Vegetable tarte tatin

This dish is a vegetable version of the classic upside-down pie, combining rice, garlic, onions and olives. You can experiment with as many different coloured vegetables as you like.

Serves 6

30ml/2 tbsp sunflower oil
25ml/1½ tbsp olive oil
1 aubergine (eggplant), sliced lengthways
1 large red (bell) pepper, seeded
    and cut into long strips
10 tomatoes
2 red shallots, finely chopped
1–2 garlic cloves, crushed
150ml/¼ pint/⅔ cup white wine
10ml/2 tsp chopped fresh basil
225g/8oz/2 cups cooked brown
    long grain rice
40g/1½oz/⅓ cup pitted black
    olives, chopped
350g/12oz vegan puff pastry
ground black pepper
salad leaves, to serve

1 Preheat the oven to 190°C/375°F/ Gas 5. Heat the sunflower oil with 15ml/1 tbsp of the olive oil in a frying pan and fry the aubergine slices, in batches if necessary, for 4–5 minutes on each side until golden brown. As each aubergine slice softens and browns, lift it out and drain on several sheets of kitchen paper to remove as much oil as possible.

Variations
• You can make individual tatins in ramekin dishes or in a muffin tray, if you prefer.
• Use a mixture of red, yellow and green (bell) peppers for extra colour.

2 Add the pepper strips to the oil remaining in the pan, turning them to coat. Cover the pan with a lid or foil and sweat the peppers over a medium-high heat for 5–6 minutes, stirring occasionally, until the pepper strips are soft and flecked with brown.

3 Slice two of the tomatoes using a sharp knife and set aside.

4 Plunge the remaining tomatoes into boiling water for 30 seconds, then drain. Peel off the skins, cut them into quarters and remove the core and seeds. Chop them roughly.

5 Heat the remaining oil in the frying pan and fry the shallots and garlic for 3–4 minutes until softened. Add the chopped tomatoes and cook for a few minutes until softened.

6 Stir in the white wine and fresh basil, with black pepper to taste. Bring the mixture to the boil, then remove from the heat and stir in the cooked rice and pitted black olives, making sure they are well distributed.

7 Arrange the tomato slices, cooked aubergine slices and peppers in a single layer over the base of a heavy, 30cm/12in shallow ovenproof dish. Spread the rice mixture on top.

8 Roll out the puff pastry to a circle slightly larger than the diameter of the dish and place it on top of the rice. Tuck the edges of the pastry circle down inside the dish.

9 Bake the tatin for 25–30 minutes, or until the pastry is golden and risen. Leave to cool slightly, then invert the tart on to a large, warmed serving plate. Serve in slices, accompanied by a leafy green salad or simply dressed lamb's lettuce or mâche.

Cook's tip
This tart would make a lovely lunch or supper dish. Serve it hot with new potatoes and a fresh green vegetable, such as mangetouts (snow peas), sugarsnap peas or green beans.

Energy 535kcal/2241kJ; Protein 8.2g; Carbohydrate 59.1g, of which sugars 8.8g; Fat 29.5g, of which saturates 1.2g; Cholesterol 0mg; Calcium 89mg; Fibre 2.6g; Sodium 521mg.

Grilled vegetable pizza

You really cannot go too far wrong with this classic mixture of grilled vegetables on home-made pizza dough. It is filling and healthy, and is a favourite with children.

Serves 6

4 plum tomatoes, skinned and chopped
60ml/4 tbsp olive oil
1 clove garlic, crushed
30ml/2 tbsp chopped fresh basil
1 courgette (zucchini), sliced
6 mushrooms, sliced
2 baby aubergines (eggplants)
   or 1 small aubergine, sliced
1 yellow (bell) pepper, seeded
   and sliced
50g/2oz/½ cup cornmeal
50g/2oz/½ cup buckwheat flour
50g/2oz/½ cup potato flour
50g/2oz/½ cup soya flour
5ml/1 tsp baking powder
2.5ml/½ tsp sea salt
50g/2oz/¼ cup non-hydrogenated vegan
   margarine or dairy-free spread
105ml/7 tbsp soya milk
salt and ground black pepper

For the cheesy topping
120ml/4fl oz rapeseed (canola) oil
120ml/4fl oz sweetened soya milk
15ml/1 tbsp tomato ketchup
5ml/1 tsp French mustard
5ml/1 tsp yeast extract or vegan
   bouillon powder

1 In a pan, place the chopped tomatoes, half the olive oil, garlic and the basil and season with salt and pepper. Simmer until reduced to a thick sauce.

2 Preheat the grill (broiler). Brush the courgette, mushrooms and aubergine slices with a little oil and place on a grill rack with the pepper slices. Cook under the grill until lightly browned, turning once.

3 Meanwhile, make the cheesy topping. With a hand blender or liquidizer, blend the oil and soya milk with the tomato ketchup, mustard and yeast extract or bouillon to form a mayonnaise consistency. If the sauce is too runny, add 15ml/1 tbsp of potato flour.

4 Meanwhile, preheat the oven to 200°C/400°F/Gas 6. Place the cornmeal, buckwheat flour, potato flour, soya flour, baking powder and salt in a large mixing bowl and stir until well combined. Lightly rub in the margarine or spread until the mixture resembles breadcrumbs, then stir in enough soya milk to make a soft dough.

5 Place the dough on a piece of baking parchment on a baking sheet and roll or gently press it out to form a 25cm/10in round, making the edges thicker than the centre.

6 Brush the dough with the remaining olive oil, then spread the thick tomato sauce evenly over the dough. Arrange the grilled vegetables on top of the tomato sauce and finish with the cheese topping. Bake for 25–30 minutes until crisp and golden brown, then serve in slices.

Energy 426kcal/1768kJ; Protein 9.2g; Carbohydrate 28.4g, of which sugars 7.1g; Fat 30.8g, of which saturates 5.9g; Cholesterol 1mg; Calcium 47mg; Fibre 4.2g; Sodium 139mg.

Vegetable moussaka with tofu topping

This vegan adaptation of the famous Greek dish is just as delicious as the traditional version made with lamb mince. An almond and tofu topping is used instead of the usual cheese sauce.

Serves 8

600g/1lb 6oz aubergines (eggplants), cut
  into 2.5cm/1in slices
30ml/2 tbsp olive oil
50ml/2fl oz/¼ cup vegetable stock
paprika and fresh basil leaves, to garnish
sea salt and ground black pepper

For the sauce
30ml/2 tbsp olive oil
2 large onions, coarsely chopped
2 garlic cloves, crushed
2 large carrots, finely chopped
4 courgettes (zucchini), sliced
200g/7oz mushrooms, sliced
2 x 400g/14oz cans chopped tomatoes
30ml/2 tbsp balsamic vinegar
15ml/1 tbsp agave syrup
5ml/1 tsp ground nutmeg

For the tofu topping
200g/7oz/1¾ cups ground almonds
350g/12oz tofu
15ml/1 tbsp soy sauce
15ml/1 tbsp lemon juice
2.5ml/½ tsp English (hot) mustard powder
30ml/2 tbsp tomato ketchup

1 Preheat the grill (broiler) to high. Place the aubergine slices in one layer on the rack. Drizzle with oil and grill (broil) for 2–3 minutes on each side until golden.

2 Make the sauce. Heat the oil in a large pan and fry the onions, garlic and carrots for 5–7 minutes. Add the remaining ingredients to the pan and season. Bring to the boil, then simmer for 20 minutes.

3 Meanwhile, make the topping. Toast the ground almonds in a heavy frying pan, without any oil, for 1–2 minutes, tossing occasionally until golden. Reserve 75g/3oz/¾ cup of the almonds. Place the remainder in a food processor or blender and add the rest of the ingredients. Process the mixture until smooth and well combined. Taste and adjust the seasoning.

4 Preheat the oven to 180°C/350°F/ Gas 4. Spread half the sauce in a 35 x 23cm/14 x 9in ovenproof dish. Add a layer of aubergine slices and spread over the remaining sauce. Finish with a layer of aubergine slices.

5 Spoon the tofu topping over the aubergine slices, ensuring it is spread evenly. Bake for about 20–25 minutes until the topping is set and has turned golden brown. Garnish with a sprinkling of paprika, fresh basil leaves and a little olive oil. Serve immediately.

Energy 768kcal/3255kJ; Protein 60.3g; Carbohydrate 109.6g, of which sugars 10.3g; Fat 13.1g, of which saturates 2.9g; Cholesterol 99mg; Calcium 357mg; Fibre 21.8g; Sodium 320mg.

Roasted courgettes and peaches with pine nuts

This distinctive dish is a colourful and delicious combination of succulent peaches and a medley of roasted vegetables. It makes a healthy dinner served with a tangy yogurt sauce, or even a tahini dressing if you prefer, and chunks of freshly baked crusty bread.

Serves 4

2 courgettes (zucchini)
2 yellow or red (bell) peppers, seeded
    and cut into wedges
100ml/3½fl oz/scant ½ cup olive oil
4–6 plum tomatoes
2 firm peaches, peeled, halved and stoned
    (pitted), then cut into wedges
30ml/2 tbsp pine nuts
salt and ground black pepper

For the yogurt sauce
500g/1¼lb/2¼ cups soya yogurt
2–3 garlic cloves, crushed
juice of ½ lemon

1 Preheat the oven to 200°C/400°F/ Gas 6. Using a vegetable peeler or a small, sharp knife, peel the courgettes lengthways in stripes like a zebra, then halve and slice them lengthways, or cut into wedges.

2 Place the courgettes and peppers in a baking dish, preferably an earthenware one. Drizzle the oil over them and sprinkle with salt, then bake in the oven for 20 minutes.

3 Take the dish out of the oven and turn the vegetables in the oil, then add the tomatoes and peaches. Bake for 20–25 minutes, until nicely browned.

4 Meanwhile, make the soya yogurt sauce. In a bowl, beat the yogurt with the garlic and lemon juice. Season with salt and pepper and set aside, or chill.

Variation
Instead of the yogurt sauce, try making a tahini dressing. Mix together 105ml/7 tbsp tahini, the juice of 1 lemon, 30ml/2 tbsp olive oil and 1 crushed garlic clove. Add water as needed to create your preferred consistency.

5 Dry-roast the pine nuts in a small, heavy pan until they turn golden brown and give off a nutty aroma. Remove from the heat.

6 When the roasted vegetables are ready, remove the dish from the oven and sprinkle the pine nuts over the top. Serve with the yogurt sauce.

Cook's tip
Try serving this dish with some pomegranate seeds for added colour and flavour.

Energy 362kcal/1507kJ; Protein 11.7g; Carbohydrate 26.7g, of which sugars 26.3g; Fat 24.1g, of which saturates 3.7g; Cholesterol 2mg; Calcium 284mg; Fibre 4.8g; Sodium 120mg.

Sweet pumpkin and peanut curry

A hearty, soothing curry perfect for autumn or winter evenings. Its cheerful colour alone will raise the spirits – and the combination of pumpkin and peanuts tastes great.

Serves 4

30ml/2 tbsp vegetable oil

4 garlic cloves, crushed

4 shallots, finely chopped

30ml/2 tbsp yellow curry paste

600ml/1 pint/2½ cups vegetable stock

2 kaffir lime leaves, torn

15ml/1 tbsp chopped fresh galangal

450g/1lb pumpkin, peeled, seeded and diced

225g/8oz sweet potatoes, diced

90g/3½oz/scant 1 cup unsalted, roasted peanuts, chopped

300ml/½ pint/1¼ cups coconut milk

90g/3½oz/1½ cups chestnut mushrooms, sliced

30ml/2 tbsp soy sauce

50g/2oz/⅓ cup pumpkin seeds, toasted, and fresh green chilli flowers, to garnish

1 Heat the oil in a wok. Add the garlic and shallots and cook over a medium heat, stirring occasionally, for 10 minutes, until softened and golden. Do not burn.

2 Add the yellow curry paste and stir-fry over medium heat for 30 seconds, until fragrant, then add the stock, lime leaves, galangal, pumpkin and sweet potatoes. Bring to the boil, stirring, then reduce the heat and simmer gently for 15 minutes.

3 Add the peanuts, coconut milk, mushrooms and soy sauce and simmer for 5 minutes more. Serve garnished with pumpkin seeds and chillies.

Variation

The well-drained vegetables from any of these curries would make a very tasty filling for a pastry or pie.

Energy 306kcal/1279kJ; Protein 9.6g; Carbohydrate 24.5g, of which sugars 11.4g; Fat 19.6g, of which saturates 3.3g; Cholesterol 0mg; Calcium 160mg; Fibre 6.4g; Sodium 409mg.

Parsnip and chickpea curry with roti

The sweet flavour of parsnips goes very well with the spices in this Indian-style vegetable stew.
Serve it with dhal and Indian roti breads to mop up the delicious sauce.

Serves 4

200g/7oz/scant 1 cup dried chickpeas,
    soaked overnight, then drained
7 garlic cloves, finely chopped
1 small onion, chopped
5cm/2in piece fresh root ginger, chopped
2 fresh green chillies, such as jalapeños
    or Serranos, seeded and finely chopped
550ml/18fl oz/2½ cups water
60ml/4 tbsp groundnut (peanut) oil
5ml/1 tsp cumin seeds
10ml/2 tsp ground coriander seeds
5ml/1 tsp ground turmeric
2.5–5ml/½–1 tsp mild chilli powder
50g/2oz/½ cup cashew nuts, toasted
    and ground
250g/9oz tomatoes, peeled and chopped
900g/2lb parsnips, cut into chunks
5ml/1 tsp ground toasted cumin seeds
juice of ½–1 lime
salt and ground black pepper

To garnish
fresh coriander (cilantro) leaves
a few cashew nuts, toasted

1 Put the chickpeas in a pan, cover
with cold water and bring to the boil.
Boil vigorously for 10 minutes, then
reduce the heat so that the water boils
steadily and cook for 1–1½ hours, or
until tender. The cooking time will
depend on how long the chickpeas
have been stored.

2 Meanwhile, make the sauce. Set
10ml/2 tsp of the garlic aside, and place
the remainder in a food processor or
blender. Add the onion, ginger and half
the chillies. Pour in 75ml/5 tbsp of the
water and process to a smooth paste.

3 Heat the oil in a large, deep frying
pan and cook the cumin seeds for
30 seconds. Stir in the coriander seeds,
turmeric, chilli powder and ground
cashew nuts. Add the ginger and chilli
paste and cook, stirring frequently, until
the water begins to evaporate. Add the
tomatoes and stir-fry until the mixture
begins to turn red-brown in colour.

4 Drain the chickpeas and add to the
pan with the parsnips and remaining
water. Season with 5ml/1 tsp salt and
black pepper. Bring to the boil, stir, then
simmer, uncovered, for 15–20 minutes,
until the parsnips are completely tender.

5 Thicken the liquid by boiling until the
sauce is reduced. Add the toasted cumin
seeds and lime juice to taste. Stir in the
reserved garlic and chilli, and heat
through. Sprinkle with the coriander
leaves and cashew nuts and serve.

Cook's tip
For a milder, less spicy flavour, use
paprika instead of chilli powder.

Variation
You could substitute red kidney
beans for chickpeas, or use carrots
and butter (lima) beans.

Energy 506kcal/2124kJ; Protein 18.4g; Carbohydrate 60.1g, of which sugars 18.2g; Fat 23.1g, of which saturates 3.4g; Cholesterol 0mg; Calcium 192mg; Fibre 17.1g; Sodium 86mg.

Tofu sausage popover

You can buy various delicious vegan tofu sausages to make this family favourite, but making them yourself is very easy and they taste simply wonderful. Serve with mashed potato.

Serves 4

For the sausages
150g/5oz/2½ cups wholemeal (whole-wheat) breadcrumbs
250g/9oz smoked tofu, drained
½ small onion, coarsely chopped
45ml/3 tbsp fresh parsley, thyme, sage or rosemary, finely chopped
10ml/2 tsp dried herbs
5ml/1 tsp Dijon mustard
5ml/1 tsp soy sauce
30ml/2 tbsp coconut oil

For the onion gravy
30ml/2 tbsp vegetable oil
1kg/2¼lb large onions, thinly sliced
105ml/7 tbsp red or dry white wine or balsamic vinegar
300ml/½ pint/1¼ cups vegetable stock
small bunch fresh thyme, woody stems removed, chopped (optional)
5ml/1 tsp yeast extract

For the batter
115g/4oz/1 cup self-raising (self-rising) flour
150ml/¼ pint/⅔ cup rapeseed (canola) oil
300ml/½ pint/1¼ cups soya milk
15ml/1 tbsp balsamic vinegar
sea salt and ground black pepper

1 Put all the sausage ingredients in a food processor, season and process until a thick paste forms. Divide the mixture into eight and roll to form sausage shapes with your hands. Arrange in a single layer on a plate, cover with clear film (plastic wrap) and chill until required.

2 Drizzle the sausages with olive oil and cook under a preheated grill (broiler) for 6–8 minutes or until pale golden brown, turning frequently.

3 To make the onion gravy, heat the oil in a large non-stick frying pan. Add the onion and cook over a medium heat for 5 minutes, until beginning to turn golden. Reduce the heat to low, then simmer for 10 minutes, stirring occasionally.

4 Add the wine or vinegar, stock, thyme and yeast extract and bring to the boil. Simmer, uncovered, for 10 minutes.

5 Make the batter. Sift the flour into a large mixing bowl and season with salt and black pepper.

6 Make a well in the middle, then add the rapeseed oil and balsamic vinegar. Mix the ingredients well. Gradually stir in the soya milk, mixing until fully incorporated, then beat until the batter is smooth.

7 Meanwhile, preheat the oven to 220°C/425°F/Gas 7. Oil a shallow ovenproof dish, then arrange the vegan sausages in the base in a single layer, leaving a little space between each.

8 Pour the batter into the dish, ensuring that it is spread evenly around the sausages. Bake in the oven for about 40–45 minutes, or until the batter is well risen and golden brown.

9 Serve the popover cut into portions with two sausages for each diner. Place the onion gravy in a jug (pitcher) and serve alongside the popover so diners can help themselves.

Variations
• The vegan sausages are also delicious cooked on their own. Grill (broil) them as in step 2 on a greased baking sheet until golden brown all over and heated through.
• Add a little finely chopped red (bell) pepper or onion, miso, or other fresh herbs to the sausage mixture.
• If you prefer wheat-free sausages, use rolled oats in place of the wholemeal breadcrumbs.

Energy 722kcal/3010kJ; Protein 17.8g; Carbohydrate 73.7g, of which sugars 17g; Fat 41.4g, of which saturates 8.5g; Cholesterol 0mg; Calcium 485mg; Fibre 5.4g; Sodium 535mg.

Tofu balls with spaghetti

This dish is popular with children and adults alike so will make a great vegan meal for the whole family. The delicious tofu balls are served with a rich and healthy vegetable sauce.

Serves 4

250g/9oz firm tofu, drained
1 onion, coarsely grated
2 garlic cloves, crushed
5ml/1 tsp Dijon mustard
15ml/1 tbsp ground cumin
1 small bunch of parsley, finely chopped
15ml/1 tbsp soy sauce
50g/2oz/½ cup ground almonds
30ml/2 tbsp olive oil
350g/12oz spaghetti
sea salt and ground black pepper
1 bunch of fresh basil, to garnish

For the sauce

15ml/1 tbsp olive oil
1 large onion, finely chopped
2 garlic cloves, chopped
1 large aubergine (eggplant), diced
2 courgettes (zucchini), diced
1 red (bell) pepper, seeded and finely chopped
15ml/1 tbsp agave syrup
400g/14oz can chopped tomatoes
200ml/7fl oz/scant 1 cup vegetable stock

1 Place the drained tofu, grated onion, crushed garlic, mustard, ground cumin, chopped parsley, soy sauce and ground almonds into a bowl. Season with sea salt and ground black pepper and mix thoroughly. Roll into about 20 walnut-sized balls, squashing the mixture together with your hands.

2 Heat the olive oil in a large frying pan, then add the tofu balls, in batches if necessary. Cook gently, turning them occasionally until brown all over. Remove the balls from the pan and set aside on a plate.

3 Heat the oil for the sauce in the same frying pan, add the onion and garlic and cook for 5 minutes, or until softened.

4 Add the aubergine, courgette, pepper and agave syrup and stir-fry for about 10 minutes until the vegetables are beginning to soften and have turned slightly brown. Season with salt and pepper.

5 Stir in the tomatoes and stock. Cover and simmer for 20 minutes, or until the sauce is rich and thickened. Just before the end of the cooking time, place the tofu balls on top of the sauce, cover and heat through for 2–3 minutes.

6 Meanwhile, cook the pasta in a large pan of salted, boiling water according to the manufacturer's instructions, then drain. Check the seasoning in the sauce before serving with the spaghetti, garnished with basil leaves.

Energy 576kcal/2422kJ; Protein 22.5g; Carbohydrate 79.4g, of which sugars 15.6g; Fat 21g, of which saturates 2.6g; Cholesterol 0mg; Calcium 425mg; Fibre 8g; Sodium 288mg.

Smoked tofu and vegetable fusilli

This quick and easy recipe is endlessly versatile. Feel free to change the ingredients to suit your own taste and what you have to hand. Try to find colourful and contrasting vegetables.

Serves 4

4 carrots, halved lengthways
   and thinly sliced diagonally
1 butternut squash, peeled, seeded
   and cut into small chunks
2 courgettes (zucchini),
   thinly sliced diagonally
1 red onion, cut into wedges
1 red (bell) pepper, seeded
   and sliced into thick strips
1 garlic bulb, cut in half horizontally
4 fresh rosemary or thyme sprigs,
   stalks removed (optional)
60ml/4 tbsp olive oil
60ml/4 tbsp balsamic vinegar
30ml/2 tbsp soy sauce
500g/1¼lb marinated deep-fried tofu
10–12 cherry tomatoes, halved
250g/9oz dried pasta, such as papardelle,
   fusilli or conchiglie
sea salt and ground black pepper

1 Preheat the oven to 220°C/425°F/ Gas 7. Place the carrots, butternut squash, courgettes, onion and pepper in a roasting pan. Add the garlic and herbs. Drizzle over the olive oil, balsamic vinegar and soy sauce.

2 Season to taste with salt and pepper and toss to coat evenly with the oil. Roast for 40–50 minutes, until the vegetables are tender and lightly browned. Toss the vegetables around once or twice during the cooking so that they all cook evenly. Add the tofu and tomatoes to the pan 10 minutes before the end of the roasting time.

3 Meanwhile, bring a large pan of lightly salted water to the boil. Add the pasta and bring the water back to the boil. Cook for about 10 minutes or until the pasta is al dente. Drain the pasta and return to the pan with a few tablespoons of the cooking water.

4 Remove the roasting pan from the oven and squeeze the garlic out of the baked skins. Toss the pasta with the vegetables, tofu and garlic. Taste and adjust the seasoning, if necessary, and serve immediately.

Cook's tip
When cooking pasta, start timing when the water returns to the boil – and boil fairly vigorously, do not simmer. Test shortly before the end of the cooking time by biting a small piece of pasta. It should feel tender, but still firm to the bite.

Energy 719kcal/3009kJ; Protein 41.2g; Carbohydrate 63.4g, of which sugars 15.4g; Fat 35.1g, of which saturates 2g; Cholesterol 0mg; Calcium 1958mg; Fibre 6.6g; Sodium 464mg.

Black bean hotpot

This dish is a nutritious and tasty mix of black beans, vibrant red and yellow peppers and orange butternut squash. The molasses imparts a rich treacly flavour to the spicy sauce.

2 Heat the oil in the pan and fry the onion and garlic for about 5 minutes until softened, stirring occasionally. Add the mustard powder, molasses, agave syrup, thyme and chilli flakes and cook for 1 minute, stirring. Stir in the black beans and spoon the mixture into a flameproof casserole.

3 Add enough water to the reserved cooking liquid to make 400ml/14fl oz/ 1⅔ cups, then mix in the bouillon powder and pour into the casserole. Bake for 25 minutes.

4 Add the peppers and squash or pumpkin and mix well. Cover, then bake for a further 45 minutes until the vegetables are tender. Serve immediately garnished with thyme.

Serves 4

225g/8oz/1¼ cups dried black beans
1 bay leaf
30ml/2 tbsp vegetable oil
1 large onion, chopped
1 garlic clove, chopped
5ml/1 tsp English (hot) mustard powder
15ml/1 tbsp blackstrap molasses
30ml/2 tbsp agave syrup
5ml/1 tsp dried thyme
2.5ml/½ tsp dried chilli flakes
5ml/1 tsp vegetable bouillon powder
1 red (bell) pepper, seeded and diced
1 yellow (bell) pepper, seeded and diced
675g/1½lb butternut squash or pumpkin,
    seeded and cut into 1cm/½in dice
salt and ground black pepper
sprigs of thyme, to garnish

1 Soak the beans overnight in plenty of water, then drain and rinse well. Place in a large pan, cover with fresh water and add the bay leaf. Bring to the boil, then boil rapidly for 10 minutes. Reduce the heat, cover, and simmer for about 30 minutes until tender. Drain, reserving the cooking water. Preheat the oven to 180°C/350°F/Gas 4.

Health benefit
Blackstrap molasses is a by-product of sugar processing and contains less sugar than treacle. It is a good source of iron, calcium, zinc, copper and chromium.

Energy 289kcal/1222kJ; Protein 15.5g; Carbohydrate 43.5g, of which sugars 13.2g; Fat 7.1g, of which saturates 1.1g; Cholesterol 0mg; Calcium 124mg; Fibre 7.9g; Sodium 17mg.

Aubergine, olive and bean tagine

Spiced with coriander, cumin, cinnamon, turmeric and chilli sauce, this Moroccan-style stew makes a filling and healthy supper dish when served with couscous or quinoa.

Serves 4

1 small aubergine (eggplant),
    cut into 1cm/½in dice
2 courgettes (zucchini), thickly sliced
60ml/4 tbsp olive oil
1 large onion, sliced
2 garlic cloves, chopped
150g/5oz/2 cups brown cap
    (cremini) mushrooms, halved
15ml/1 tbsp ground coriander
10ml/2 tsp cumin seeds
15ml/1 tbsp ground cinnamon
10ml/2 tsp ground turmeric
225g/8oz new potatoes, quartered
600ml/1 pint/2½ cups passata
    (bottled strained tomatoes)
15ml/1 tbsp tomato purée (paste)
15ml/1 tbsp chilli sauce
75g/3oz/scant ½ cup ready-to-eat
    unsulphured dried apricots
400g/14oz/scant 3 cups canned butter
    (lima) beans, drained and rinsed
salt and ground black pepper
15ml/1 tbsp chopped fresh coriander
    (cilantro), to garnish
couscous or quinoa, to serve (optional)

3 Meanwhile, heat the remaining oil in a large, heavy pan and cook the onion and garlic for about 5 minutes until softened, stirring occasionally. Add the mushrooms and cook for 3 minutes until just tender. Add the spices and cook for 1 minute more, stirring, to allow the flavours to mingle.

4 Add the potatoes and cook for about 3 minutes, stirring. Pour in the passata, tomato purée and 150ml/¼ pint/⅔ cup water, cover, and cook for 10 minutes or until the sauce begins to thicken.

5 Add the aubergine, courgettes, chilli sauce, apricots and butter beans. Season and cook, partially covered, for 10–15 minutes until the potatoes are tender. Add extra water if the tagine is too dry. Serve with couscous or quinoa, if using, and garnish with coriander.

Health benefit
Butter beans, like many pulses, contain a good amount of protein, potassium and iron.

1 Sprinkle salt over the aubergine and courgettes and leave for 30 minutes. Rinse and pat dry with a dish towel.

2 Heat the grill (broiler) to high. Arrange the courgettes and aubergine on a baking sheet and toss in 30ml/2 tbsp of the olive oil. Grill (broil) for about 20 minutes, turning the vegetables occasionally, until they are tender and evenly browned.

Energy 359kcal/1509kJ; Protein 13.9g; Carbohydrate 45g, of which sugars 19.3g; Fat 15g, of which saturates 2.1g; Cholesterol 0mg; Calcium 123mg; Fibre 9.7g; Sodium 597mg.

Carrot and nut biryani

This simple and wholesome rice dish, based on the traditional biryani from India, makes a great meal for the whole family. Try adding some wild or cultivated mushrooms, if you like.

Serves 4

15–30ml/1–2 tbsp rapeseed (canola) oil
1 onion, chopped
1 garlic clove, crushed
1 large carrot, coarsely grated
225g/8oz/generous 1 cup brown
　basmati rice, soaked
5ml/1 tsp cumin seeds
10ml/2 tsp ground coriander
10ml/2 tsp black mustard seeds (optional)
4 green cardamom pods
450ml/¾ pint/scant 2 cups vegetable stock
1 bay leaf
75g/3oz/¾ cup walnuts and cashew nuts
salt and ground black pepper
fresh parsley or coriander (cilantro),
　to garnish

1 Heat the rapeseed oil in a large, shallow frying pan and gently fry the onion for 3–4 minutes. Add the garlic and carrot and fry for 3 minutes. Drain the rice and then add to the pan along with the spices. Cook for a further 1–2 minutes, stirring to coat the grains in the oil.

2 Pour in the stock, add the bay leaf and season well. Bring to the boil, then lower the heat, cover and simmer very gently for 10–12 minutes.

3 Remove the pan from the heat without lifting the lid. Leave to stand for about 5 minutes, then check the rice. If it is cooked, there will be small steam holes on the surface of the rice. Remove and discard the bay leaf and the cardamom pods.

4 Stir in the nuts and check the seasoning. Spoon on to a platter, garnish with the parsley or coriander and serve immediately.

Variations
• Use whichever nuts you prefer in this dish – even unsalted peanuts taste good, although almonds, cashew nuts or pistachios are more exotic.
• If you use mushrooms, add them right at the beginning while frying the onions.

Energy 364kcal/1517kJ; Protein 8.9g; Carbohydrate 52.4g, of which sugars 3.3g; Fat 13.2g, of which saturates 2.3g; Cholesterol 0mg; Calcium 33mg; Fibre 1.3g; Sodium 61mg.

Tofu and wild rice salad

This dish tastes wonderful on its own. Tofu is rich in protein and low in fat and makes a nutritious addition to a vegan meal, while also providing a wide range of essential vitamins and minerals.

Serves 4

175g/6oz/scant 1 cup basmati rice
50g/2oz/generous ¼ cup wild rice
250g/9oz firm tofu, drained and cubed
25g/1oz preserved lemon, finely chopped
  (see Cook's tip)
20g/¾oz bunch of fresh parsley, chopped

For the dressing
1 garlic clove, crushed
10ml/2 tsp clear agave syrup
10ml/2 tsp of the preserved lemon juice
15ml/1 tbsp cider vinegar
15ml/1 tbsp olive oil
1 small fresh red chilli, seeded
  and finely chopped
5ml/1 tsp harissa paste (optional)
ground black pepper

1 Cook the basmati rice and the wild rice in separate pans until tender. The basmati will take about 10–15 minutes to cook, while the wild rice will take 45–50 minutes. (It is possible to buy packets of ready-mixed long grain and wild rice. This takes 25 minutes to cook because the tough outer skin of the wild rice has been broken.)

2 Meanwhile, whisk together all the dressing ingredients in a small bowl. Add the tofu, stir to coat and leave to marinate for about 20 minutes while the rice cooks.

3 Drain the two rices, rinse well under cold water and drain again. Place in a large mixing bowl.

4 Mix the tofu, dressing, lemon and parsley into the rice. Serve immediately.

Cook's tip
Preserved lemons are available from Middle Eastern delicatessens or from some supermarkets.

Energy 284kcal/1185kJ; Protein 9.6g; Carbohydrate 47.6g, of which sugars 2.4g; Fat 5.8g, of which saturates 0.7g; Cholesterol 0mg; Calcium 355mg; Fibre 0.6g; Sodium 7mg.

Vegetable paella

The success of a paella depends on two of the essential ingredients: the rice and the stock. Always taste the stock before adding it to rice – this is your chance to add some wine, a bit of a stock cube, or even miso or soy sauce to boost the flavour of the dish.

3 Add the remaining oil to the pan and cook the onion for 3–4 minutes until beginning to soften. Add the garlic and cook for a further 2 minutes.

4 Add the peppers, green beans and mushrooms to the pan. Cook, stirring occasionally, for about 3 minutes until just beginning to soften.

5 Add the drained rice and cook for 1–2 minutes, stirring to ensure it is coated in the oil. Add the aubergine slices and stir to combine. Add the chilli and season to taste. Pour in the stock and add the peas and parsley.

6 Bring to boiling point, cover and cook over a low heat for 20–25 minutes, checking the liquid level toward the end (the rice should absorb the liquid, but not burn).

7 When the rice is tender, turn off the heat, cover the pan and leave to stand for 10 minutes for the remaining liquid to be absorbed. Garnish with parsley or coriander and serve immediately.

Serves 4

1 large aubergine (eggplant)
45ml/3 tbsp olive oil
2 onions, quartered and sliced
2 garlic cloves, finely chopped
1 red (bell) pepper, halved, seeded and sliced
1 yellow (bell) pepper, halved, seeded and sliced
200g/7oz/ 1⅓ cup fine green beans, halved
115g/4oz/1½ cups brown cap (cremini) mushrooms, halved
300g/11oz/1½ cups paella rice, washed and drained
1 dried chilli, seeded and crumbled
1 litre/1¾ pints/4 cups vegetable stock
115g/4oz/1 cup peas
60ml/4 tbsp chopped fresh parsley
salt and ground black pepper
fresh parsley or coriander (cilantro) leaves, to garnish

1 Halve the aubergine lengthways, then cut it into slices. Spread them out in a large colander or on a draining board, sprinkle with salt and leave for about 30 minutes. Rinse under cold running water and pat dry with kitchen paper.

2 Heat 30ml/2 tbsp olive oil in a large pan over a high heat. Cook the aubergine until slightly golden, turning once. Transfer to kitchen paper to drain.

Variation
Almost any roughly chopped or sliced vegetables can be used in this dish. Broccoli, carrots, cauliflower, courgettes (zucchini) and okra are all suitable – or try using frozen corn.

Energy 388kcal/1646kJ; Protein 13.5g; Carbohydrate 78.8g, of which sugars 7.5g; Fat 3.6g, of which saturates 0.9g; Cholesterol 0mg; Calcium 57mg; Fibre 8.5g; Sodium 299mg.

Couscous with dried fruit and nuts

This dish of couscous mixed with dates, raisins and nuts would typically form part of a celebration meal in Morocco. It is delicious served on its own, but for a more substantial meal it is especially good served alongside a spicy tagine made with chunky vegetables.

Serves 6

500g/1¼lb/3 cups couscous
600ml/1 pint/2½ cups warm water
5ml/1 tsp salt
pinch of saffron threads
45ml/3 tbsp sunflower oil
30ml/2 tbsp olive oil
115g/4oz/½ cup ready-to-eat
  dried apricots, cut into slivers
75g/3oz/½ cup dried dates, chopped
75g/3oz/generous ½ cup
  seedless raisins
115g/4oz/⅔ cup blanched
  almonds, cut into slivers
75g/3oz/½ cup pistachio nuts
10ml/2 tsp ground cinnamon
45ml/3 tbsp caster (superfine) sugar

1 Preheat the oven to 180°C/350°F/ Gas 4. Put the couscous in a bowl. Mix together the water, salt and saffron and pour it over the couscous, stirring. Leave to stand for 10 minutes. Add the sunflower oil and, using your fingers, rub it through the grains. Set aside.

2 Heat the olive oil in a large pan and stir in the apricots, dates, raisins, most of the almonds (reserve some for the garnish) and pistachio nuts.

3 Cook until the raisins plump up, then transfer into the couscous and mix well. Spoon the couscous into an ovenproof dish and cover with foil. Bake in the oven for 20 minutes, until heated through.

4 Toast the reserved sliced almonds. Pile the couscous in a mound on a serving dish and sprinkle with the cinnamon and sugar in stripes down the mound. Sprinkle the toasted almonds over the top and serve.

Energy 576kcal/2403kJ; Protein 12.5g; Carbohydrate 73g, of which sugars 29.4g; Fat 27.8g, of which saturates 3.1g; Cholesterol 0mg; Calcium 102mg; Fibre 4.2g; Sodium 74mg.

Pumpkin stuffed with pistachio, saffron and apricot pilaff

Pumpkins are not just for Halloween or making a classic pumpkin pie. They also make ideal cooking vessels, to be filled with aromatic pilaffs, as in this recipe, or perhaps with a quinoa-based dish: either way, they make an interesting and unusual centrepiece. This sumptuous and wholesome fruit and nut pilaff is great for special occasions, such as part of a celebration feast or a vegan dinner party.

Serves 4–6

1 medium pumpkin, weighing about
   1.2kg/2½lb
225g/8oz/generous 1 cup long grain
   brown rice, well rinsed
30–45ml/2–3 tbsp olive oil
15ml/1 tbsp soya margarine
pinch of saffron threads
5ml/1 tsp coriander seeds
2–3 strips of orange rind, finely sliced
45–60ml/3–4 tbsp shelled pistachio nuts
30–45ml/2–3 tbsp dried cranberries
175g/6oz/¾ cup ready-to-eat
   dried apricots, chopped
1 bunch of fresh basil,
   leaves loosely torn
1 bunch each of fresh coriander
   (cilantro), mint and flat leaf parsley,
   coarsely chopped
salt and ground black pepper
lemon wedges and soya yogurt,
   to serve

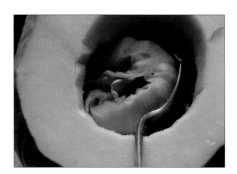

1 Preheat the oven to 200°C/400°F/ Gas 6. Wash the pumpkin and cut off the stalk end to use as a lid. Scoop all the seeds out of the middle with a metal spoon, and pull out the stringy bits. Replace the lid, put the pumpkin on a baking tray and bake for 1 hour.

2 Meanwhile, put the rice into a heavy pan and pour in just enough water to cover. Add a pinch of salt and bring the water to the boil, then lower the heat and partially cover the pan.

3 Simmer the rice for 10–12 minutes, until all the water has been absorbed and the grains of rice are cooked but still have a bite.

Cook's tip
You could use roasted pumpkin seeds instead of pistachio nuts.

4 Heat the oil and margarine in a wide, heavy pan. Stir in the saffron, coriander seeds, orange rind, pistachios, cranberries and apricots, then toss in the cooked rice and mix well. Season with salt and pepper.

5 Turn off the heat, cover the pan with a dish towel and press the lid tightly on top. Leave the pilaff to steam for about 10 minutes, then toss in the herbs.

6 Take the pumpkin out of the oven. Lift off the lid and spoon the pilaff into the cavity. Put the lid back on and pop it back in the oven for about 20 minutes.

7 To serve, remove the lid and slice a round off the top of the pumpkin. Place the ring on a plate and spoon some pilaff in the middle. Continue slicing and filling on individual plates until all the pumpkin and pilaff are used up. Serve with lemon wedges and soya yogurt.

Energy 345kcal/1443kJ; Protein 9.9g; Carbohydrate 50.1g, of which sugars 18.6g; Fat 12g, of which saturates 2.6g; Cholesterol 5mg; Calcium 299mg; Fibre 9.6g; Sodium 93mg.

salads and side dishes

Separate side dishes enable you to add variety and colour to the table, as well as complementary flavours to your main course. It is a nice idea for your guests to be able to serve their own side dishes, adding as much or as little as they want. You may want to serve two or three side dishes, depending on your choice of main course. Traditional side dishes include Scalloped Potatoes with Garlic, and Kale with Mustard Dressing, and a range of fresh and vibrant salads includes Sea Vegetable Salad, and Avocado and Grapefruit Salad.

Moroccan carrot salad

Carrots have been renowned for hundreds of years for their health-giving properties and high vitamin A content. They are a very popular and versatile vegetable used in a wide variety of dishes such as this African salad, in which they are cooked before being tossed in a vinaigrette.

Serves 4–6

3–4 carrots, thinly sliced
5ml/1 tsp agave syrup
3–4 garlic cloves, chopped
1.5ml/¼ tsp ground cumin, or to taste
juice of ½ lemon
30–45ml/2–3 tbsp extra virgin olive oil
15–30ml/1–2 tbsp red wine vinegar or fruit
    vinegar, such as raspberry
30ml/2 tbsp chopped fresh coriander (cilantro)
    leaves or a mixture of coriander and parsley
salt and ground black pepper

1 Cook the carrots by either steaming or boiling in lightly salted water until they are just tender but not soft. Drain, leave for a few moments to dry, then put in a large bowl.

2 Add the agave syrup, garlic, cumin, lemon juice, olive oil and vinegar and toss together until all the carrots are evenly coated. Add the herbs and season. Serve warm or chilled.

Energy 53kcal/220kJ; Protein 0.6g; Carbohydrate 4.2g, of which sugars 3.9g; Fat 3.9g, of which saturates 0.6g; Cholesterol 0mg; Calcium 29mg; Fibre 1.6g; Sodium 15mg.

Beetroot and red onion salad

There is a wide range of beetroots available – most are an intense red colour but there are also pink and yellow varieties, which are well worth seeking out. This tangy and refreshing salad looks especially attractive when made with a mixture of the red and yellow types.

Serves 6

500g/1¼lb small red and yellow
   beetroot (beets)
75ml/5 tbsp water
60ml/4 tbsp olive oil
90g/3½oz/scant 1 cup walnut or
   pecan halves
10ml/2 tsp agave syrup
30ml/2 tbsp walnut oil
15ml/1 tbsp balsamic vinegar
5ml/1 tsp soy sauce
5ml/1 tsp grated orange rind
2.5ml/½ tsp ground roasted coriander seeds
5–10ml/1–2 tsp orange juice
1 red onion, halved and very thinly sliced
15–30ml/1–2 tbsp chopped fresh fennel
75g/3oz watercress or mizuna leaves
handful of baby red chard or beetroot
   leaves (optional)
sea salt and ground black pepper

3 Meanwhile, heat 15ml/1 tbsp of the olive oil in a small frying pan and cook the walnuts or pecans until they begin to brown.

4 Add 5ml/1 tsp of agave syrup to the pan and cook, stirring, until the nuts begin to caramelize. Season with salt and lots of black pepper, then turn the nuts out on to a plate and leave to cool.

5 In a jug (pitcher) or small bowl, whisk together the remaining olive oil, the walnut oil, vinegar, soy sauce, orange rind and ground roasted coriander seeds to make the dressing. Season with salt and pepper to taste and mix in the rest of the agave syrup. Whisk in orange juice to taste.

6 Separate the red onion slices into half-rings and add them to the strips of beetroot. Add the dressing and toss thoroughly to mix.

7 When ready to serve, toss the salad with the fennel, watercress or mizuna and red chard or beetroot leaves, if using. Transfer to individual bowls or plates and sprinkle with the caramelized nuts. Serve immediately.

1 Preheat the oven to 180°C/350°F/Gas 4. Place the beetroot in a shallow ovenproof dish just large enough to hold them in a single layer, and add the water. Cover the dish tightly with a close-fitting lid or foil and bake for about 1–1½ hours, or until the beetroot are just cooked and tender.

2 Allow the beetroot to cool. Once cooled, peel them, then slice them into roughly equal strips and place in a large bowl. Add about 15ml/1 tbsp of the olive oil to the bowl and mix thoroughly until the beetroot strips are well coated in oil.

Energy 239kcal/991kJ; Protein 3.3g; Carbohydrate 8.2g, of which sugars 7.2g; Fat 21.7g, of which saturates 2.3g; Cholesterol 0mg; Calcium 50mg; Fibre 2.6g; Sodium 121mg.

Sea vegetable salad

This salad is a fine example of the traditional Japanese idea of eating: look after your appetite and your health at the same time. Seaweed is a nutritious, alkaline food which is rich in fibre and iodine. Its unique flavours are a great complement to vegetable and tofu dishes.

Serves 4

5g/⅛oz each dried wakame, dried arame and
   dried hijiki seaweeds
130g/4½oz enokitake mushrooms
2 spring onions (scallions)
a few ice cubes
½ cucumber, cut lengthways
250g/9oz mixed salad leaves

For the marinade
15ml/1 tbsp rice vinegar
10ml/2 tsp soy sauce

For the dressing
60ml/4 tbsp rice vinegar
7.5ml/1½ tsp toasted sesame oil
15ml/1 tbsp shoyu
15ml/1 tbsp water with a pinch of dashi-no-
   moto (dashi stock granules)
2.5cm/1in piece fresh root ginger, grated

1 First rehydrate the seaweeds. Soak the dried wakame seaweed for about 10 minutes in one bowl of water and, in a separate bowl of water, soak the dried arame and hijiki seaweeds together for 30 minutes.

2 Using a sharp knife, trim off the hard end of the enokitake mushroom stalks and discard. Cut the bunch in half and separate the stems.

3 Make the spring onion curls for the garnish. Slice the spring onions into thin strips about 4cm/1½in long, then place the strips into a bowl of cold water with a few ice cubes added. This will cause the onion strips to curl up. Drain the onions thoroughly. Slice the cucumber into thin, half-moon shapes.

4 Cook the wakame and enokitake in boiling water for 2 minutes, then add the arame and hijiki for a few seconds. Immediately remove from the heat. Drain and sprinkle over the vinegar and soy sauce while still warm. Chill.

5 Mix the dressing ingredients in a bowl. Arrange the mixed salad leaves in a large bowl with the cucumber on top, then add the seaweed and enokitake mixture. Decorate the salad with spring onion curls and serve with the dressing.

Health benefit
The iodine in the seaweed helps to keep your thyroid gland in balance.

Energy 33kcal/139kJ; Protein 2.1g; Carbohydrate 2.2g, of which sugars 1.8g; Fat 1.9g, of which saturates 0.3g; Cholesterol 0mg; Calcium 48mg; Fibre 1.4g; Sodium 237mg.

Avocado and grapefruit salad

This is a light, refreshing lunchtime salad. The buttery texture of the avocados combines with the tanginess of the grapefruit to make the perfect summer dish. Serve it as an appetizer to a light main course of falafel or pakora, served with warm pitta bread.

Serves 4

90ml/6 tbsp olive oil
30ml/2 tbsp white wine vinegar
1 pink grapefruit
2 large ripe avocados
1 cos or romaine lettuce, separated
   into leaves
salt and ground black pepper

1 Using a balloon whisk or a fork, whisk the olive oil and white wine vinegar together in a large bowl, season to taste with salt and ground black pepper and vigorously whisk again.

2 Slice the top and bottom off the pink grapefruit. Peel the fruit by running a small knife all around it, between the peel and flesh. Make sure all the bitter pith is removed.

3 Hold the grapefruit over the bowl containing the dressing and cut carefully between the membranes, so that all the segments fall into the bowl. Squeeze the remaining pulp over the bowl to extract all the juice.

4 Run a knife around the length of the avocados. Twist the sides in opposite directions to separate the halves. Use a large spoon to remove the stone (pit), then peel the halves. Slice the flesh and cover the slices with the dressing, to stop them from discolouring.

5 Tear the lettuce into pieces and add them to the bowl. Toss gently until evenly coated in the dressing. Adjust the seasoning to taste and serve.

Variation
Try other fruit combinations. Mango and strawberries go well together, as do papaya and limes.

Energy 151kcal/625kJ; Protein 1.1g; Carbohydrate 5.6g, of which sugars 5.2g; Fat 13.9g, of which saturates 2.4g; Cholesterol 0mg; Calcium 24mg; Fibre 1.9g; Sodium 13mg.

Mayan pumpkin salad

In this Latin American salad, red wine vinegar brings out the sweetness of the pumpkin, which is then combined with plenty of fresh parsley, which is rich in iron and calcium.

Serves 4

1 large red onion, peeled and very
   thinly sliced
200ml/7fl oz/scant 1 cup olive oil
60ml/4 tbsp red wine vinegar
675g/1½lb pumpkin, peeled and cut into
   4cm/1½in pieces
40g/1½oz/¾ cup fresh flat leaf parsley
   leaves, chopped
salt and ground black pepper

Variation

Try replacing the pumpkin with sweet potatoes. Wild rocket (arugula) or coriander (cilantro) can be used instead of the parsley.

1 Mix the red onion, olive oil and red wine vinegar in a large bowl. Stir well until thoroughly combined.

2 Put the pumpkin pieces in a large pan of cold salted water. Bring to the boil, then lower the heat and simmer gently for 15–20 minutes or until the pumpkin is tender, then drain.

3 Immediately add the drained pumpkin to the bowl containing the dressing. Toss lightly with your hands until the pumpkin is well coated. Leave to cool.

4 Stir in the chopped parsley, cover with clear film (plastic wrap) and chill. Allow the salad to come back to room temperature before serving.

Energy 404kcal/1663kJ; Protein 1.7g; Carbohydrate 5.2g, of which sugars 4g; Fat 42g, of which saturates 6.1g; Cholesterol 0mg; Calcium 73mg; Fibre 2.4g; Sodium 4mg.

Asparagus and orange salad

A slightly unusual combination of ingredients with a simple dressing based on good quality fruity olive oil, tender spears of asparagus, juicy oranges and ripe tomatoes.

Serves 4

225g/8oz asparagus, trimmed
   and cut into 5cm/2in lengths
2 large oranges
2 ripe tomatoes, cut into eighths
50g/2oz cos or romaine lettuce leaves
30ml/2 tbsp extra virgin olive oil
2.5ml/½ tsp sherry vinegar
   or balsamic vinegar
ground black pepper

1 Cook the asparagus in boiling, lightly salted water for 3–4 minutes, until just tender. The cooking time may vary according to the size of the asparagus stems. Drain and refresh under cold water, then leave on one side to cool.

2 Finely grate the rind from half an orange and reserve. Peel both the oranges and cut them into segments. Squeeze the juice from the membrane and reserve.

3 Put the asparagus, orange segments, tomatoes and lettuce into a salad bowl.

4 Mix together the oil and vinegar, and add 15ml/1 tbsp of the reserved orange juice and 5ml/1 tsp of the grated rind. Season with salt and black pepper.

5 Just before serving, pour the dressing over the salad and mix gently to coat all the salad ingredients in the dressing.

Cook's tip
The bottom of the asparagus stalk is usually hard and woody – and becomes more so with age – so it will probably need to be cut off with a sharp knife. However, if you are using short, slender asparagus stems, sometimes called 'spruce', then it may not be necessary to trim them.

Energy 102kcal/424kJ; Protein 2.9g; Carbohydrate 9.3g, of which sugars 9.2g; Fat 6.1g, of which saturates 0.9g; Cholesterol 0mg; Calcium 58mg; Fibre 2.9g; Sodium 9mg.

Orange and olive salad

This is a refreshing salad to enjoy with a main course or it is equally good added to a selection of buffet or picnic dishes. It goes particularly well with home-made pizza.

Serves 6

5 large oranges
90g/3½oz/½ cup black olives
1 red onion, thinly sliced
1 large fennel bulb, thinly sliced,
    feathery tops reserved
15ml/1 tbsp chopped fresh mint,
    plus a few extra sprigs to garnish
15ml/1 tbsp chopped fresh coriander
    (cilantro), plus extra to garnish

For the dressing
60ml/4 tbsp olive oil
10ml/2 tsp lemon juice
2.5ml/½ tsp ground toasted
    coriander seeds
2.5ml/½ tsp orange flower water
salt and ground black pepper

1 Peel the oranges with a sharp knife, making sure you remove all the white pith, and cut them into 5mm/¼in slices. Remove any pips (seeds) and work over a bowl to catch all the orange juice. Set the juice aside for adding to the salad dressing.

2 Pit the olives, if you like. In a bowl, toss the orange slices, onion and fennel together with the olives, chopped fresh mint and coriander.

3 Make the dressing. In a bowl, whisk together the olive oil, 15ml/1 tbsp of the reserved orange juice and the lemon juice. Add the ground toasted coriander seeds and season to taste with salt and pepper. Mix thoroughly.

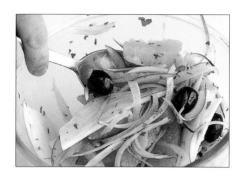

4 Toss the dressing into the salad, cover and leave to stand in a cool place for 30–60 minutes.

5 To serve, drain off any excess dressing and place the salad in a serving dish or bowl. Sprinkle with the chopped herbs and reserved fennel tops, and sprinkle with the orange flower water.

Energy 150kcal/629kJ; Protein 3g; Carbohydrate 18.9g, of which sugars 16.4g; Fat 7.6g, of which saturates 1.1g; Cholesterol 0mg; Calcium 102mg; Fibre 3.8g; Sodium 292mg.

Celery and coconut salad with lime

This salad is a delicious balance of the crunchy, slightly bitter celery with sweet and creamy coconut. The addition of lime juice makes this dish particularly refreshing.

Serves 3–4

45–60ml/3–4 tbsp coconut cream
2 garlic cloves, crushed
5ml/1 tsp grated lime rind
juice of 1 lime
8 long celery sticks, grated
    (leaves reserved for the garnish)
flesh of ½ fresh coconut, grated
salt and ground black pepper
a few sprigs of fresh flat leaf parsley,
    to garnish

1 Pour the coconut cream into a large bowl. Add the garlic and mix until well combined. Stir in the lime rind and juice and season with salt and plenty of ground black pepper.

2 Fold the grated celery and coconut into the bowl with the dressing, then set aside for 15–20 minutes to let the celery juices weep. Do not leave it for too long or it will become watery.

3 To serve, spoon the salad into a bowl and garnish with celery and parsley.

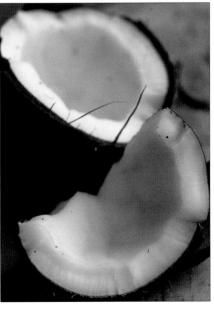

Energy 126kcal/521kJ; Protein 2.1g; Carbohydrate 2.9g, of which sugars 2.9g; Fat 11.9g, of which saturates 10.1g; Cholesterol 0mg; Calcium 63mg; Fibre 3.6g; Sodium 69mg.

Chopped vegetable salad

This classic summer salad lends itself to endless variety: try adding olives, diced beetroot or potatoes. You can also omit the chilli, vary the herbs, or use lime or lemon instead of vinegar.

Serves 4–6

1 each red, green and yellow (bell)
    pepper, seeded
1 carrot
1 cucumber
6 tomatoes
3 garlic cloves, finely chopped
3 spring onions (scallions), thinly sliced
30ml/2 tbsp chopped fresh coriander
    (cilantro) leaves
30ml/2 tbsp each chopped fresh dill,
    parsley and mint leaves
½–1 hot fresh chilli, seeds removed
    and chopped (optional)
45–60ml/3–4 tbsp extra virgin olive oil
juice of 1–1½ lemons
salt and ground black pepper

1 Using a sharp knife, finely dice the red, green and yellow peppers, carrot, cucumber and tomatoes. Place them in a large mixing bowl and toss gently with your hands to mix.

2 Add the garlic, spring onions, coriander, dill, parsley, mint and chilli, if using, to the chopped vegetables and toss together to combine.

3 Pour the olive oil and lemon juice over the vegetables, season with salt and pepper to taste and toss together. Chill before serving.

Variation
Try adding a handful of capers to the salad for extra piquancy.

Cucumber, potato and pepper salad

A great, refreshing and piquant salad for any time of year. It is hearty enough to enjoy on its own or as a side dish to a larger meal, such as part of a buffet selection. Try to use the best quality olives that are available. The black Kalamata style olives from Greece will be ideal.

Serves 4

1 large cucumber, thinly sliced
2 cold, boiled potatoes, sliced
1 each red, yellow and green (bell) pepper,
    seeded and thinly sliced
300g/11oz/1¼ cups pitted olives
½–1 hot fresh chilli, chopped, or
    2–3 shakes of cayenne pepper
3–5 garlic cloves, chopped
3 spring onions (scallions), sliced
    or 1 red onion, finely chopped
60–90ml/4–6 tbsp extra virgin olive oil
15–30ml/1–2 tbsp white wine vinegar
juice of ½ lemon, or to taste
15–30ml/1–2 tbsp chopped fresh
    mint leaves
15–30ml/1–2 tbsp chopped fresh
    coriander (cilantro) leaves
salt (optional)

1 Arrange the cucumber, potato and pepper slices and the pitted olives on a serving plate or in a dish.

2 Sprinkle the chopped fresh chilli or cayenne pepper over the salad and season with salt, if you like. (Bear in mind that olives tend to be very salty so you may not need to add any extra salt – taste before seasoning.)

3 Sprinkle the garlic, onions, olive oil, vinegar and lemon juice over the salad. Chill before serving, sprinkled with the chopped mint and coriander leaves.

Variation
Serve the salad garnished with sliced cooked beetroot (beet).

Energy 116kcal/485kJ; Protein 3g; Carbohydrate 12.2g, of which sugars 11.7g; Fat 6.5g, of which saturates 1.1g; Cholesterol 0mg; Calcium 43mg; Fibre 3.8g; Sodium 21mg.
Energy 159kcal/656kJ; Protein 1.9g; Carbohydrate 5.8g, of which sugars 5.6g; Fat 14.4g, of which saturates 2.1g; Cholesterol 0mg; Calcium 46mg; Fibre 2.4g; Sodium 13mg.

Avocado guacamole

Often served as a dip with corn chips, this highly nutritious salsa is also great served alongside a main course. It is made from avocados, onion and tomatoes spiked with fresh chilli, crushed garlic, toasted cumin seeds and fresh lime juice. Half mash and half dice the avocados for a more interesting, chunky texture.

Serves 4

2 large ripe avocados
1 small red onion, finely chopped
1 fresh red or green chilli, seeded and
    very finely chopped
1 garlic clove, crushed
finely shredded rind of ½ lime and juice
    of 1–1½ limes
225g/8oz tomatoes, seeded and chopped
30ml/2 tbsp roughly chopped fresh
    coriander (cilantro)
2.5–5ml/½–1 tsp ground toasted
    cumin seeds
15ml/1 tbsp olive oil
ground black pepper
lime wedges and fresh coriander (cilantro)
    sprigs, to garnish
lightly salted corn chips, to serve (optional)

1 Cut one of the avocados in half and lift out and discard the stone (pit). Scrape the flesh from both halves into a bowl and mash it roughly with a fork.

2 Add the onion, chilli, garlic, lime rind, tomatoes and coriander and stir well. Add the ground cumin seeds and pepper to taste, then stir in the olive oil.

3 Halve and stone the remaining avocado. Dice the flesh and stir it into the guacamole.

4 Squeeze in fresh lime juice to taste, mix well, then cover and leave to stand for 15 minutes so that the flavour develops. Serve with lime wedges and garnish with fresh coriander sprigs.

Energy 187kcal/771kJ; Protein 2.4g; Carbohydrate 4.7g, of which sugars 3.3g; Fat 17.6g, of which saturates 3.5g; Cholesterol 0mg; Calcium 41mg; Fibre 4g; Sodium 14mg.

Cactus salsa

Often seen lurking in the background of Hollywood western movies, nopales are the tender, fleshy leaves, or paddles, of an edible cactus known variously as the cactus pear or the prickly pear cactus. They grow wild in Mexico and some areas of North America, but they are also cultivated and can be bought from specialist food stores and some large supermarkets.

Serves 4

2 fresh red fresno chillies
250g/9oz nopales (cactus paddles)
3 spring onions (scallions)
3 garlic cloves, peeled
½ red onion
100g/3¾oz fresh tomatillos
2.5ml/½ tsp salt
150ml/¼ pint/⅔ cup cider vinegar

1 Spear the chillies on a long-handled metal skewer and roast them over the flame of a gas burner until the skins blister and darken. Do not let the flesh burn. Alternatively, dry fry them in a griddle pan until the skins are scorched. Place the roasted chillies in a strong plastic bag and tie the top to keep the steam in. Set aside for 20 minutes.

2 Remove the chillies from the bag and peel off the skins. Cut off the stalks, then slit the chillies and scrape out the seeds. Chop the chillies roughly and set them aside.

3 Carefully remove the thorns from the nopales. Wearing gloves or holding each cactus paddle in turn with kitchen tongs, cut off the bumps that contain the thorns with a sharp knife.

4 Cut off and discard the thick base from each cactus paddle. Rinse the paddles well and cut them into strips, then cut the strips into small pieces.

5 Bring a large pan of lightly salted water to the boil. Add the cactus paddle pieces, spring onions and garlic. Boil for 10–15 minutes, until the paddle pieces are just tender.

6 Drain the mixture in a colander, rinse under cold running water to remove any remaining stickiness, then drain again. Discard the spring onions and garlic.

7 Chop the red onion and the tomatillos finely. Place in a bowl and add the cactus and chillies.

8 Spoon the mixture into a preserving jar, add the salt, pour in the vinegar and seal. Chill for at least a day, turning the jar occasionally to ensure that the nopales are marinated. The salsa will keep in the refrigerator for 10 days.

Energy 18kcal/79kJ; Protein 1.5g; Carbohydrate 2.8g, of which sugars 2.4g; Fat 0.3g, of which saturates 0g; Cholesterol 0mg; Calcium 72mg; Fibre 1.5g; Sodium 6mg.

Black bean salsa

This salsa has a fabulously striking appearance. It is rare to find a predominantly black dish and it provides a wonderful contrast to the more common reds and greens on the plate. The pasado chillies add a subtle citrus flavour. Leave the salsa for a day or two after preparing it to allow all the wonderful flavours to develop and mingle fully.

3 Spear the fresno chillies on a long-handled metal skewer and roast them over the flame of a gas burner until the skins blister and darken. Do not let the flesh burn. Alternatively, dry fry them in a griddle pan until the skins are scorched. Then place the roasted chillies in a strong plastic bag and tie the top to keep the steam in. Set aside for 20 minutes.

4 Meanwhile, chop the red onion finely. Remove the chillies from the bag and peel off the skins. Slit them, remove the seeds and chop them finely.

5 Transfer the beans into a bowl and add the onion and both types of chilli. Stir in the lime rind and juice, beer, oil and coriander. Season with salt and mix well. Chill before serving.

Serves 4

175g/6oz/1 cup black beans, soaked
   overnight in water to cover
1 pasado chilli
2 fresh red fresno chillies
1 red onion
grated rind and juice of 1 lime
30ml/2 tbsp Mexican beer (optional)
15ml/1 tbsp olive oil
small bunch of fresh coriander (cilantro),
   finely chopped
salt

1 Drain the beans and place in a large pan. Pour in water to cover and place the lid on the pan. Bring to the boil, then simmer for 40 minutes or until tender. They should still have a little bite. Drain, rinse under cold water, then drain again and set aside until cold.

2 Soak the pasado chilli in hot water for about 10 minutes until softened. Drain, remove the stalk, then slit the chilli and scrape out the seeds with a small sharp knife. Chop the flesh finely.

Cook's tip
Mexican beer is a light beer; Sol and Tecate are popular varieties.

Energy 109kcal/461kJ; Protein 6.6g; Carbohydrate 14g, of which sugars 1.1g; Fat 3.4g, of which saturates 0.5g; Cholesterol 0mg; Calcium 49mg; Fibre 2.7g; Sodium 9mg.

Spinach and raisins with pine nuts

It is impossible to have too many vegan recipes that show new and delicious ways to prepare spinach. This makes a change from the classic creamy garlicky spinach dishes. It makes an excellent filling wrapped up in filo pastry to serve as finger food at a party. The combination of raisins, nuts and tangy onions make this a truly delectable accompaniment to a larger meal.

Serves 4

60ml/4 tbsp raisins
1kg/2¼lb fresh spinach leaves, washed
45ml/3 tbsp olive oil
6–8 spring onions (scallions), thinly sliced
    or 1–2 small yellow or white onions,
    finely chopped
60ml/4 tbsp pine nuts
salt and ground black pepper

1 Put the raisins into a small bowl and pour over boiling water to cover. Leave to stand for about 10 minutes until plumped up, then drain.

2 Steam or cook the spinach in a pan over a medium-high heat, with only the water that clings to the leaves after washing, for 1–2 minutes until the leaves are bright green and wilted. Remove from the heat and drain well. Leave to cool.

3 When the spinach has cooled, chop roughly with a sharp knife.

Variations
• Add goji berries instead of raisins.
• Try using apricot kernels instead of the pine nuts.

4 Heat the oil in a frying pan over a medium-low heat, then lower the heat further and add the spring onions or onions. Fry for about 5 minutes, or until soft, then add the spinach, raisins and pine nuts. Raise the heat and cook for 2–3 minutes to warm through. Season with salt and ground black pepper to taste and serve immediately.

Energy 206kcal/855kJ; Protein 5.8g; Carbohydrate 15.5g, of which sugars 11.1g; Fat 13.8g, of which saturates 1.6g; Cholesterol 0mg; Calcium 228mg; Fibre 3.4g; Sodium 218mg.

Charred artichokes with lemon oil

There is no reason why you have to miss out on summer barbecues as a vegan. Many vegetables make great kebabs, and these young artichokes are delicious cooked over charcoal. They are also good roasted in the oven, as here. Store any surplus in olive oil in the refrigerator.

Serves 2–4

15ml/1 tbsp lemon juice or white wine vinegar
2 globe artichokes
45ml/3 tbsp olive oil
sea salt
sprigs of fresh flat leaf parsley, to garnish

For the lemon oil dip
12 garlic cloves, unpeeled
1 lemon
45ml/3 tbsp extra virgin olive oil

Cook's tip
This is a perfect dish to have alongside a vegan pizza.

1 Preheat the oven to 200°C/400°F/ Gas 6. Stir the lemon juice or vinegar into a bowl of cold water.

2 Cut each artichoke lengthways into wedges. Pull the hairy choke out from the centre of each wedge and drop the pieces into the acidulated water.

3 Drain the artichokes and place in a roasting pan with the garlic cloves. Toss in the oil. Sprinkle with salt and roast for 40 minutes, stirring once or twice, until the artichokes are tender.

4 Meanwhile, make the dip. Pare away two strips of rind from the lemon and scrape away any pith. Place the rind in a pan with water to cover. Simmer for 5 minutes, then drain, refresh in cold water and chop roughly.

5 Arrange the artichokes on a plate and set aside to cool for 5 minutes. Flatten the garlic cloves so that the flesh pops out of the skins.

6 Transfer the garlic flesh to a bowl, mash to a purée, then add the lemon rind. Squeeze the lemon juice into the bowl. Stir in the extra virgin olive oil and, using a fork or whisk, stir until the mixture is well combined.

7 Serve the artichokes warm. Garnish them with the parsley and serve the lemon dip alongside.

Energy 165kcal/679kJ; Protein 1.3g; Carbohydrate 2.6g, of which sugars 0.8g; Fat 16.7g, of which saturates 2.4g; Cholesterol 0mg; Calcium 24mg; Fibre 1.1g; Sodium 31mg.

Marinated mushrooms

These succulent mushrooms make a fabulous alternative to traditional garlic mushrooms.
Experiment with different varieties of the many wild mushrooms now available in food stores.
Serve with plenty of home-made wholemeal bread to mop up the delicious juices.

Serves 4

30ml/2 tbsp olive oil
1 small onion, very finely chopped
1 garlic clove, finely chopped
15ml/1 tbsp tomato purée (paste)
50ml/2fl oz/¼ cup sherry
50ml/2fl oz/¼ cup vegetable stock
2 cloves
225g/8oz/3 cups button (white) mushrooms
salt and ground black pepper
chopped fresh parsley, to garnish

Cook's tip
In Spain, wild mushrooms, known
as setas, are served in this way.

1 Heat the oil in a pan. Add the onion
and garlic and cook until soft. Stir in the
tomato purée, sherry, stock and the
cloves and season with salt and pepper.

2 Bring to the boil, cover and simmer
gently for 45 minutes, adding more
water if it becomes too dry.

3 Add the mushrooms to the pan, then
cover and allow to simmer for about
5 minutes.

4 Remove from the heat and allow to
cool, still covered. Chill in the refrigerator
overnight. Serve the mushrooms cold,
sprinkled with fresh parsley.

Energy 80kcal/329kJ; Protein 1.4g; Carbohydrate 2.1g, of which sugars 1.7g; Fat 5.8g, of which saturates 0.9g; Cholesterol 0mg; Calcium 9mg; Fibre 0.9g; Sodium 14mg.

Cauliflower with tomatoes and cumin

This recipe makes an excellent side dish to serve alongside vegetable kebabs or tofu burgers.
It is also a great addition to a buffet or served with other tapas dishes.

Serves 4

30ml/2 tbsp sunflower or olive oil
1 onion, chopped
1 garlic clove, crushed
1 small cauliflower, broken into florets
5ml/1 tsp cumin seeds
a good pinch of ground ginger
4 tomatoes, peeled, seeded and quartered
15–30ml/1–2 tbsp lemon juice (optional)
30ml/2 tbsp chopped fresh coriander
   (cilantro) (optional)
salt and ground black pepper

Variation
Whole cherry tomatoes can also be
used in this dish instead of the
tomato slices.

1 Heat the oil in a heavy pan, add the
onion and garlic. Stir-fry for 2–3 minutes
until the onion is softened. Add the
cauliflower and stir-fry for 2–3 minutes
until the cauliflower is flecked with brown.

2 Add the cumin seeds and ginger, fry
briskly for 1 minute, and then add the
tomato wedges, 175ml/6fl oz/¾ cup
water and some salt and pepper.

3 Bring to the boil and then reduce the
heat, cover with a plate or with foil and
simmer for 6–7 minutes, until the
cauliflower is just tender.

4 Stir in a little lemon juice, if using, to
sharpen the flavour. Taste and adjust
the seasoning if necessary. Sprinkle
over the chopped coriander, if using,
and serve immediately.

Roast vegetable salad

Roasting vegetables in the oven helps to concentrate all the delicious flavours and adds a lovely
hint of smokiness. This versatile salad can be served hot with practically anything.

Serves 4

8 chestnut mushrooms
2–3 courgettes (zucchini)
1 Spanish (Bermuda) onion
2 red (bell) peppers
16 cherry tomatoes
2 garlic cloves, chopped
pinch of cumin seeds
5ml/1 tsp fresh thyme or 4–5 torn basil leaves
60ml/4 tbsp olive oil
juice of ½ lemon
5–10ml/1–2 tsp harissa or Tabasco sauce
fresh thyme sprigs, to garnish

Cook's tip
Try roasting the vegetables with
added chunks of tofu for some
extra protein.

1 Preheat the oven to 220°C/425°F/
Gas 7. Halve the mushrooms. Top and
tail the courgettes and cut into long
strips. Cut the onion into thin wedges.
Halve the peppers, discard the seeds
and core, and cut into bitesize chunks.

2 Place the vegetables in a cast iron
dish or roasting pan, add the tomatoes,
garlic, cumin seeds and thyme or basil.
Sprinkle with olive oil and toss to coat.

3 Place the pan in the oven and leave
for 25–30 minutes until the vegetables
are very soft and tender and slightly
charred at the edges.

4 Put the lemon juice into a bowl and
stir in the harissa or Tabasco sauce.
Pour over the vegetables and gently
toss to coat evenly. Serve immediately
while still hot, garnished with the fresh
thyme sprigs.

Energy 106kcal/441kJ; Protein 4.5g; Carbohydrate 7.3g, of which sugars 6.5g; Fat 6.7g, of which saturates 1g; Cholesterol 0mg; Calcium 32mg; Fibre 3g; Sodium 19mg.
Energy 319kcal/1343kJ; Protein 8.8g; Carbohydrate 49.6g, of which sugars 8g; Fat 10.8g, of which saturates 1.6g; Cholesterol 0mg; Calcium 34mg; Fibre 4g; Sodium 9mg.

Cauliflower with garlic crumbs

This dish makes a great appetizer served with chutney or a spicy fruit sauce. It also perfectly complements filo pastry dishes or can be eaten as a healthy lunch with a crisp green salad.

2 Heat 60–75ml/4–5 tbsp of the olive or vegetable oil in a frying pan. Add the breadcrumbs and cook over a medium heat, tossing and turning, until evenly browned and crisp.

3 Add the garlic to the pan. Stir once or twice for 2 minutes. Remove the breadcrumbs and garlic from the pan and set aside.

4 Heat the remaining oil in the pan, then add the cauliflower, mashing and breaking it up a little as it lightly browns in the oil. (Do not overcook, but just cook lightly in the oil.)

5 Add the garlic breadcrumbs to the pan and cook, stirring, until well combined and some of the cauliflower is still holding its shape. Season with salt and pepper and serve hot or warm.

Serves 4–6

600ml/1 pint/2½ cups vegetable stock
1 large cauliflower, cut into bitesize florets
90–120ml/6–8 tbsp olive or vegetable oil
130g/4½oz/2¼ cups dry white or wholemeal (whole-wheat) breadcrumbs
3–5 garlic cloves, thinly sliced or chopped
salt and ground black pepper

Variation
You can swap the breadcrumbs for rolled oats, if you prefer.

1 Pour the vegetable stock into a large pan and bring to the boil. Add a pinch of salt and the cauliflower florets. Simmer until just tender. Drain and leave to cool.

Cook's tip
Try serving this dish as they do in Italy: with cooked pasta such as spaghetti or rigatoni.

Energy 244kcal/1016kJ; Protein 8.9g; Carbohydrate 18.8g, of which sugars 2.2g; Fat 15.3g, of which saturates 3.8g; Cholesterol 10mg; Calcium 162mg; Fibre 1.7g; Sodium 280mg.

Spiced greens with hemp seeds

Here is a perfect way to enliven your greens. It works well with crunchy cabbages but is also good for kale and other purple sprouting leaves – even Brussels sprout tops can be used.

Serves 4

1 medium cabbage, or the equivalent in
    quantity of your chosen green vegetable
15ml/1 tbsp groundnut (peanut) oil
5ml/1 tsp grated fresh root ginger
2 garlic cloves, crushed
2 shallots, finely chopped
2 red chillies, seeded and finely sliced
30ml/2 tbsp hemp seeds
salt and ground black pepper

Cook's tip
This dish is the perfect way to encourage children to get their fill of nutritious leafy green vegetables.

1 Remove any tough outer leaves from the cabbage then quarter it and remove the core. Shred the leaves.

2 Pour the groundnut oil into a large pan and as it heats stir in the ginger and garlic. Add the shallots and as the pan becomes hotter add the chillies.

3 Add the greens and toss to mix thoroughly. Cover the pan and reduce the heat. Cook, shaking the pan occasionally, for about 3–5 minutes. Remove the lid and increase the heat to dry off the steam. Add the hemp seeds, season with salt and pepper and cook for a further minute. Serve immediately.

Energy 77kcal/322kJ; Protein 2.6g; Carbohydrate 9.9g, of which sugars 9.4g; Fat 3.1g, of which saturates 0.5g; Cholesterol 0mg; Calcium 90mg; Fibre 3.9g; Sodium 13mg.

Kale with mustard dressing

This is a winter dish from Ireland, where sea kale is a popular vegetable. Its pale green fronds have a slightly nutty taste. Use curly kale or a dark green cabbage if sea kale is unavailable, although you will need to boil it briefly for a few minutes before chilling and serving.

Serves 4

250g/9oz sea kale or curly kale
45ml/3 tbsp light olive oil
5ml/1 tsp wholegrain mustard
15ml/1 tbsp white wine vinegar
5ml/1 tsp agave syrup
salt and ground black pepper

1 Wash the kale, drain, then trim it and tear into pieces. Cook briefly if needed.

2 Whisk the oil into the mustard in a bowl. When it is blended completely, whisk in the white wine vinegar. It should begin to thicken.

3 Season the mustard dressing to taste with agave syrup, a little salt and plenty of ground black pepper.

4 Toss the sea kale in the dressing and serve immediately.

Energy 99kcal/409kJ; Protein 2.1g; Carbohydrate 1.9g, of which sugars 1.9g; Fat 9.3g, of which saturates 1.3g; Cholesterol 0mg; Calcium 82mg; Fibre 1.9g; Sodium 27mg.

Sweet potato and beetroot with coconut

This dish benefits from the wonderful sweetness that develops when the vegetables are oven roasted. The potatoes and beetroot are perfectly complemented by the savoury onions, and the aromatic coriander, coconut, ginger and garlic paste adds an irresistible spicy fragrance.

Serves 4–6

30ml/2 tbsp groundnut (peanut) oil
   or mild olive oil
450g/1lb sweet potatoes, peeled
   and cut into thick strips or chunks
4 beetroot (beets), cooked, peeled
   and cut into wedges
450g/1lb small red or yellow onions, halved
5ml/1 tsp coriander seeds, lightly crushed
3–4 small whole fresh red chillies
salt and ground black pepper
chopped fresh coriander (cilantro), to garnish

For the paste
2 large garlic cloves, chopped
1–2 green chillies, seeded and chopped
15ml/1 tbsp chopped fresh root ginger
45ml/3 tbsp chopped fresh coriander (cilantro)
75ml/5 tbsp coconut milk
30ml/2 tbsp groundnut (peanut) oil
   or mild olive oil
grated rind of ½ lime
5ml/1 tsp agave syrup

1 First make the spicy paste. Put the garlic, chillies, ginger, coriander and coconut milk in a food processor or blender. Process the mixture until it is thoroughly combined.

2 Transfer the paste into a small mixing bowl. Pour in the groundnut or olive oil, add the lime rind and the agave syrup. Whisk the mixture with a fork until all the ingredients are well combined. Meanwhile, preheat the oven to 200°C/ 400°F/Gas 6.

3 Heat the oil in a roasting pan in the oven for 5 minutes. Add the sweet potatoes, beetroot, onions and coriander seeds, tossing them in the hot oil. Roast for 10 minutes.

4 Stir the paste and the whole red chillies into the vegetables in the pan. Season well with salt and ground black pepper. Gently toss the vegetables to coat them thoroughly with the paste.

5 Roast the vegetables for a further 25–35 minutes, or until the sweet potatoes and onions are fully cooked and tender. Stir 2–3 times during cooking to prevent the paste from sticking to the pan.

6 Serve the vegetables immediately, garnished with fresh coriander.

Energy 272kcal/1143kJ; Protein 4.4g; Carbohydrate 39.8g, of which sugars 19.1g; Fat 11.8g, of which saturates 1.7g; Cholesterol 0mg; Calcium 98mg; Fibre 6.3g; Sodium 122mg.

Grilled leek and fennel salad with tomato dressing

This is an excellent salad to make when young leeks are in season and ripe tomatoes are full of flavour. It makes a fabulous accompaniment to a vegan pizza or grilled vegetable kebabs.

Serves 6

675g/1½lb leeks
2 large fennel bulbs
120ml/4fl oz/½ cup extra virgin olive oil
2 shallots, chopped
150ml/¼ pint/⅔ cup dry white wine
   or white vermouth
5ml/1 tsp fennel seeds, crushed
6 fresh thyme sprigs
2–3 bay leaves
good pinch of dried red chilli flakes
350g/12oz ripe tomatoes, peeled,
   seeded and diced
5ml/1 tsp sun-dried tomato paste (optional)
salt and ground black pepper
75g/3oz/¾ cup small black olives,
   to serve

1 Cook the leeks in boiling salted water for 4–5 minutes. Use a slotted spoon to remove them and place in a colander to drain thoroughly. Leave to cool. Reserve the cooking water in the pan. Squeeze out any excess water from the leeks and cut into 7.5cm/3in lengths.

Cook's tip

When buying fennel, look for rounded bulbs; they have a better shape for this dish. The flesh should be crisp and white, with no signs of bruising. Avoid specimens with broken leaves or with brown or dried-out patches.

2 Trim the fennel bulbs, reserving any tops for the garnish, if you like, and cut the bulbs either into thin slices or into thicker wedges, according to taste.

3 Cook the fennel in the reserved cooking water for about 5 minutes, then drain thoroughly and toss with 30ml/2 tbsp of the olive oil. Season to taste with black pepper.

4 Heat a ridged cast-iron griddle until very hot. Arrange the leeks and fennel on the griddle and cook, turning once or twice, until they have deep brown stripes across them. Remove the vegetables from the griddle, place them in a large shallow dish and set aside.

5 Place the remaining olive oil, the shallots, white wine or vermouth, crushed fennel seeds, thyme, bay leaves and chilli flakes in a large pan. Bring the mixture to the boil over a medium heat. Lower the heat and simmer for about 10 minutes.

6 Add the diced tomatoes to the pan and cook briskly for about 5–8 minutes, or until they have reduced and the consistency of the mixture has thickened slightly.

7 Add the sun-dried tomato paste, if using. Taste and adjust the seasoning if necessary.

8 Pour the tomato dressing over the leeks and fennel in the dish. Toss all the vegetables gently to mix in the tomato dressing, then set the dish aside to cool.

9 When ready to serve, stir the salad once more and then sprinkle over the fennel tops, if using. Serve with black olives.

Health benefit

Leeks provide useful levels of iron as well as the antioxidants carotene and vitamins E and C.

Energy 193kcal/801kJ; Protein 2.8g; Carbohydrate 6.7g, of which sugars 5.9g; Fat 14.7g, of which saturates 2.2g; Cholesterol 0mg; Calcium 53mg; Fibre 4.6g; Sodium 297mg.

Hot vegetable and tarragon salad

This delicious side dish contains a variety of tender young vegetables, which are just lightly cooked to bring out their different flavours and to retain as much nutrient value as possible. The tarragon adds a wonderful depth of flavour to this bright, fresh dish.

Serves 4

5 spring onions (scallions)
30ml/2 tbsp olive oil
1 garlic clove, crushed
115g/4oz asparagus tips
115g/4oz mangetouts (snow peas), trimmed
115g/4oz broad (fava) beans
2 Little Gem (Bibb) lettuces
5ml/1 tsp finely chopped fresh tarragon
ground black pepper

1 Cut the spring onions into quarters lengthways with a sharp knife. Heat the olive oil in a large frying pan, add the spring onions and the crushed garlic and fry gently over a medium-low heat for a few minutes, until softened.

2 Add the asparagus tips, mangetouts and broad beans to the pan and stir around. Mix well, covering all the vegetables with oil.

3 Just cover the base of the pan with water, season with pepper, and allow to simmer gently for a few minutes.

4 Cut the lettuce into quarters with a sharp knife and add to the frying pan. Cook for 3 minutes, then remove the pan from the heat.

5 Transfer the cooked vegetables to a warmed serving dish, add the chopped tarragon, and serve immediately.

Energy 124kcal/515kJ; Protein 5.1g; Carbohydrate 6.8g, of which sugars 3.5g; Fat 8.7g, of which saturates 3.8g; Cholesterol 13mg; Calcium 62mg; Fibre 3.9g; Sodium 44mg.

Garlic and potato mash

These creamy mashed potatoes are perfect with all kinds of roast or grilled vegetables – and although it seems a lot of garlic is used, the flavour is deliciously sweet and subtle when cooked in this way. Try adding some nori seaweed flakes for a tasty and nutritious twist.

Serves 6–8

2 garlic bulbs, separated into
  cloves, unpeeled
115g/4oz/½ cup soya margarine
1.3kg/3lb baking potatoes
120–175ml/4–6fl oz/½–¾ cup soya milk
salt and white pepper

1 Bring a small pan of water to the boil over a high heat. Add the garlic cloves and boil for about 2–3 minutes, then drain and peel.

2 In a heavy frying pan, melt half the margarine over a low heat. Add the blanched garlic cloves, then cover and cook gently for 20–25 minutes until very tender and just golden, shaking the pan and stirring occasionally. Do not allow the garlic to scorch or brown.

3 Remove the pan from the heat. Spoon the garlic and any margarine into a blender or a food processor and process until smooth. Transfer to a small bowl, cover the surface to prevent a skin forming and set aside.

4 Peel and quarter the potatoes, place in a large pan and add enough cold water to just cover them. Salt the water generously and bring to the boil over a high heat. Reduce the heat and simmer the potatoes until tender.

5 Drain the potatoes then work through a food mill or press through a sieve (strainer) back into the pan.

6 Return the pan to a medium heat and, using a wooden spoon, stir the potatoes for about 1–2 minutes to dry them out completely. Remove the pan from the heat.

7 Warm the milk over a medium-high heat until bubbles form. Gradually beat the soya milk, remaining margarine and reserved garlic purée into the potatoes, then season with salt, if needed, and white pepper. Serve immediately.

Energy 261kcal/1093kJ; Protein 5g; Carbohydrate 33.3g, of which sugars 3.8g; Fat 12.8g, of which saturates 7.9g; Cholesterol 32mg; Calcium 43mg; Fibre 2.4g; Sodium 118mg.

Roasted rosemary new potatoes

These new potatoes, flavoured with fresh rosemary and lots of garlic, are excellent with vegetable stews but equally perfect with a Sunday nut roast, pie or even a salad.

Serves 4

800g/1¾lb small new potatoes
5 garlic cloves, peeled and bruised
3 rosemary sprigs
30ml/2 tbsp olive oil
sea salt and ground black pepper

Health benefit
Garlic is particularly valued for its ability to boost the immune system.

Cook's tip
Garlic cloves lose their pungency when roasted, becoming sweeter.

1 Preheat the oven to 200°C/400°F/ Gas 6. Put the potatoes, garlic and rosemary in a roasting pan and drizzle with the oil to coat. Season well.

2 Bake for 40–45 minutes, shaking halfway through cooking, until the potatoes are crisp on the outside and soft in the centre.

3 Discard the rosemary and garlic from the pan, if you wish, and serve.

Variation
Shallots can be roasted in the same way. Cook for 35 minutes or until they are tender.

Orange-glazed carrots

Naturally sweet carrots, combined with a glossy sweet mustard glaze, make a healthy and delicious accompaniment to all sorts of vegan main courses.

Serves 4

450g/1lb carrots, cut into
   thick matchsticks
25g/1oz/2 tbsp soya margarine
15ml/1 tbsp olive oil
1 garlic clove, crushed
15ml/1 tbsp chopped fresh
   rosemary leaves
5ml/1 tsp Dijon mustard
10ml/2 tsp agave syrup

1 Steam the carrot matchsticks in a steamer over a pan of boiling water for 2–4 minutes.

Health benefit
Carrots are a rich source of beta carotene, the plant form of vitamin A. One carrot can supply the body with enough of this vitamin for an entire day.

2 Heat the soya margarine and oil in a heavy pan, add the garlic and rosemary and cook, stirring, for 1 minute or until the garlic is golden brown. Ensure that it does not burn, otherwise it will taste bitter and spoil the sweetness of the dish.

3 Add the carrots, Dijon mustard and agave syrup to the pan, and cook, stirring constantly, for 2–3 minutes or until the carrots are only just tender. Serve immediately.

Energy 691kcal/2900kJ; Protein 24.9g; Carbohydrate 85.3g, of which sugars 6.4g; Fat 30.2g, of which saturates 10.6g; Cholesterol 39mg; Calcium 410mg; Fibre 4.2g; Sodium 620mg.
Energy 122kcal/507kJ; Protein 1g; Carbohydrate 11.1g, of which sugars 10.4g; Fat 8.6g, of which saturates 2.8g; Cholesterol 1mg; Calcium 32mg; Fibre 2.7g; Sodium 85mg.

Stir-fried pineapple and ginger

This dish makes an interesting accompaniment to tofu dishes. If the idea seems strange, think of it as resembling a fresh mango chutney, but with pineapple as the principal ingredient.

Serves 4

1 pineapple
15ml/1 tbsp vegetable oil
2 garlic cloves, finely chopped
2 shallots, finely chopped
5cm/2in piece fresh root ginger,
   peeled and finely shredded
30ml/2 tbsp light soy sauce
juice of ½ lime
1 large fresh red chilli, seeded
   and finely shredded

Variation
Peaches or nectarines can be substituted for the diced pineapple.

1 Trim and peel the pineapple. Cut out the core and dice the flesh.

2 Heat the oil in a wok or frying pan. Stir-fry the garlic and shallots over a medium heat for 2–3 minutes, until golden. Do not let the garlic burn or the dish will taste bitter.

3 Add the pineapple. Stir-fry for about 2 minutes, or until the pineapple cubes start to turn golden on the edges.

4 Add the ginger, soy sauce, lime juice and shredded chilli. Toss together until well mixed. Cook over a low heat for a further 2 minutes, then serve.

Energy 89kcal/375kJ; Protein 0.7g; Carbohydrate 14.1g, of which sugars 13.7g; Fat 3.7g, of which saturates 0.4g; Cholesterol 0mg; Calcium 27mg; Fibre 1.8g; Sodium 3mg.

Scalloped potatoes with garlic

This tasty side dish goes perfectly with chunky vegetable stews or can be enjoyed as a light lunch on its own. Cooking the potatoes in stock gives them a deliciously rich flavour.

Serves 4–6

900g/2lb waxy potatoes, peeled and
   thinly sliced
450ml/¾ pint/scant 2 cups vegetable stock
15g/½oz/1 tbsp soya margarine or
   dairy-free spread
1 large onion, very finely sliced into rings
2–4 garlic cloves, finely chopped
2.5ml/½ tsp dried thyme
60ml/4 tbsp rolled oats
30ml/2 tbsp olive oil
sea salt and ground black pepper

1 Preheat the oven to 180°C/350°F/ Gas 4. Bring the stock to the boil in a pan. Add the potatoes and simmer for 6–7 minutes until just tender but not breaking apart.

2 Grease a baking tray with the soya margarine or spread. Place a layer of onions in the tray, then sprinkle over a little of the chopped garlic, thyme, salt and pepper.

3 Carefully arrange an overlapping layer of potato slices on top of the onion mixture. Continue to layer the ingredients in the dish in this way until all the onions, garlic, herbs and potatoes are used up, finishing with a layer of sliced potatoes.

Variation
To vary the flavour, try substituting chopped rosemary or sage in place of the dried thyme.

4 Sprinkle over the oats, drizzle with the oil and season with salt and pepper. Bake for about 30 minutes until crispy and golden on top. Serve immediately.

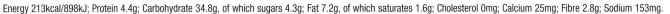

Energy 213kcal/898kJ; Protein 4.4g; Carbohydrate 34.8g, of which sugars 4.3g; Fat 7.2g, of which saturates 1.6g; Cholesterol 0mg; Calcium 25mg; Fibre 2.8g; Sodium 153mg.

Potatoes with chilli beans

East meets West in this delicious side dish, with potatoes and beans given a distinctly Chinese twist. It can also be enjoyed as a light meal on its own when you fancy a dish with a little kick.

Serves 4

4 medium firm or waxy potatoes,
    cut into thick chunks
30ml/2 tbsp sunflower or groundnut
    (peanut) oil
3 spring onions (scallions), sliced
1 large fresh red chilli, seeded
    and thinly sliced
2 garlic cloves, crushed
400g/14oz can red kidney beans, drained
30ml/2 tbsp soy sauce
15ml/1 tbsp sesame oil
salt and ground black pepper
15ml/1 tbsp sesame seeds,
    to garnish
chopped fresh coriander (cilantro)
    or parsley, to garnish

1 Cook the potatoes in boiling water until they are just tender. Take care not to overcook them. Drain and set aside.

2 Heat the oil in a large frying pan or wok over a medium-high heat. Add the spring onions and chilli and stir-fry for about 1 minute, then add the garlic and stir-fry for a few seconds longer.

3 Add the potatoes, stirring well, then the beans and finally the soy sauce and sesame oil.

4 Season to taste with salt and pepper and continue to cook the vegetables until they are heated through. Sprinkle with the sesame seeds and the coriander or parsley and serve immediately.

Tomato and potato bake

An adaptation of a classic Greek dish, which is usually cooked on top of the stove. This recipe has a richer, deeper flavour as it is stove cooked first before being baked in the oven.

Serves 4

120ml/4fl oz/½ cup olive oil
1 large onion, finely chopped
3 garlic cloves, crushed
4 large ripe tomatoes, peeled,
    deseeded and chopped
1kg/2¼lb firm or waxy potatoes
salt and ground black pepper
flat leaf parsley, to garnish

1 Preheat the oven to 180°C/350°F/ Gas 4. Heat the oil in a flameproof casserole. Fry the onion and garlic for 5 minutes until beginning to soften and just starting to brown.

Cook's tip
Make sure that the potatoes are completely coated in the oil for even cooking.

2 Add the tomatoes to the pan, season with salt and pepper and cook, stirring constantly, for 1 minute.

3 Cut the potatoes into wedges. Add to the pan. Cook, stirring, for 10 minutes. Season again and cover with a lid.

4 Place the casserole in the middle of the oven and bake for 45–50 minutes until the potatoes are tender. Serve immediately, garnished with parsley.

Energy 272kcal/1141kJ; Protein 9.7g; Carbohydrate 34.8g, of which sugars 5.7g; Fat 11.4g, of which saturates 1.6g; Cholesterol 0mg; Calcium 107mg; Fibre 7.6g; Sodium 936mg.
Energy 415kcal/1735kJ; Protein 6g; Carbohydrate 50.5g, of which sugars 11.2g; Fat 22.4g, of which saturates 3.3g; Cholesterol 0mg; Calcium 45mg; Fibre 4.7g; Sodium 37mg.

Escalivada

The Catalan name of this celebrated dish means 'baked over embers', but it can also be very successfully baked in the oven and is just as delicious. Cooking vegetables using this method is great for vegans as it helps to concentrate their flavours, resulting in an extremely tasty dish.

Serves 4

2–3 courgettes (zucchini)
1 large fennel bulb
1 Spanish (Bermuda) onion
2 large red (bell) peppers
450g/1lb butternut squash
6 garlic cloves, unpeeled
75ml/5 tbsp olive oil
juice of ½ lemon
pinch of cumin seeds, crushed
4 sprigs fresh thyme
4 medium tomatoes
salt and ground black pepper

1 Preheat the oven to 220°C/425°F/ Gas 7. Cut the courgettes lengthways into four pieces.

2 Cut the fennel into wedges of a similar size. Slice the onion lengthways into chunks. Halve and seed the peppers, and slice thickly lengthways.

3 Cut the squash into thick chunks. Smash the garlic cloves with the flat of a knife, but leave the skins on.

4 Choose a roasting pan into which all the vegetables will fit in roughly one layer. Put in all the vegetables except the tomatoes.

5 Mix together the oil and lemon juice. Pour over the vegetables and toss to coat. Sprinkle with the cumin seeds, season and add the thyme sprigs. Roast for 20 minutes.

6 Remove the pan and gently toss the vegetables. Cut the tomatoes into wedges and add to the pan. Cook for 15–20 minutes, or until the vegetables are tender and slightly charred around the edges. Serve immediately.

Variation
You can vary the vegetables according to what is in season. Baby vegetables are excellent roasted. Look out for tiny fennel and young leeks in season.

Energy 209kcal/864kJ; Protein 4.6g; Carbohydrate 14.3g, of which sugars 13g; Fat 15.1g, of which saturates 2.4g; Cholesterol 0mg; Calcium 86mg; Fibre 5.6g; Sodium 17mg.

Aubergines in red wine

Apparently it was the Arabs who introduced this strange looking vegetable to Spain, where it was cooked with the Arab flavourings of cumin and garlic. Later, dishes similar to French ratatouille became popular using aubergine as one of the main ingredients.

Serves 4

1 large aubergine (eggplant)
60–90ml/4–6 tbsp olive oil
2 shallots, thinly sliced
4 tomatoes, quartered
2 garlic cloves, thinly sliced
60ml/4 tbsp red wine
30ml/2 tbsp chopped fresh parsley,
  plus extra to garnish
30–45ml/2–3 tbsp extra virgin
  olive oil (if serving cold)
salt and ground black pepper

1 Slice the aubergine into 1cm/½in rounds. Place them in a large colander and sprinkle with 5–10ml/1–2 tsp salt. Leave to drain for 30 minutes.

2 Rinse the aubergine slices well, then press between several layers of kitchen paper to remove any excess liquid.

3 Heat 30ml/2 tbsp of the oil in a large frying pan until smoking. Add one layer of aubergine slices and fry, turning once, until golden brown. Transfer to a plate covered with kitchen paper. Heat more oil in the pan and fry the second batch in the same way.

4 Heat 15ml/1 tbsp of oil in the pan and cook the shallots for 5 minutes until golden.

5 Cut the aubergine slices into strips. Add these to the shallots with the tomatoes, garlic and wine. Cover the pan and simmer for 30 minutes, stirring from time to time.

6 Stir in the parsley, and check the seasonings, adjusting if necessary. Garnish with a little more parsley and serve immediately if you want it hot. To serve cold, drizzle a little extra virgin olive oil over the dish and bring it to room temperature before serving.

Energy 137kcal/569kJ; Protein 1.6g; Carbohydrate 4.8g, of which sugars 4.6g; Fat 11.7g, of which saturates 1.7g; Cholesterol 0mg; Calcium 34mg; Fibre 2.8g; Sodium 15mg.

Sichuan spiced aubergine

This straightforward yet versatile vegan dish is based on the style of cooking in the Chinese province of Sichuan. It can be served hot, warm or cold, as the occasion demands. Topped with a sprinkling of toasted sesame seeds, it is easy to prepare and tastes absolutely wonderful.

Serves 4–6

2 aubergines (eggplants), total weight
    about 600g/1lb 6oz, cut into
    large chunks
15ml/1 tbsp salt
5ml/1 tsp chilli powder, or to taste
75–90ml/5–6 tbsp sunflower oil
15ml/1 tbsp rice wine
100ml/3½fl oz/scant ½ cup water
salt and ground black pepper
a few toasted sesame seeds,
    to garnish

For the chilli sauce

15–30ml/1–2 tbsp chilli paste
2 garlic cloves, crushed
15ml/1 tbsp dark soy sauce
15ml/1 tbsp rice vinegar
10ml/2 tsp light soy sauce

1 Put all the chilli sauce ingredients in a jug (pitcher) and mix well. Set aside.

2 Place the aubergine chunks on a plate, sprinkle them with the salt and leave to stand for 15–20 minutes.

3 Rinse well, drain and dry thoroughly on kitchen paper. Toss the aubergine cubes in the chilli powder.

4 Heat the oil in a wok. Add the aubergine chunks and the rice wine. Cook, stirring constantly, until the aubergine chunks start to brown. Stir in the water, cover the wok and steam for 2–3 minutes. Add the chilli sauce and cook for 2 minutes. Season to taste, then transfer to a serving dish, garnish with sesame seeds and serve.

Kan Shao green beans

This is a delicious Sichuan-inspired dish suitable for vegans. Kan Shao means 'dry-cooked' – meaning no stock or water is used. The slim green beans, usually available all the year round, are ideal in this quick and easy recipe. Other long green beans can be substituted.

Serves 6

175ml/6fl oz/¾ cup sunflower oil
450/1lb fresh green beans, topped,
    tailed and cut in half
1cm/½in piece fresh root ginger,
    peeled and cut into matchsticks
5ml/1 tsp agave syrup
10ml/2 tsp light soy sauce
salt and ground black pepper

> **Variation**
> This simple recipe works just as well with various other fresh green vegetables. Try replacing the green beans with baby asparagus spears or okra, cut into chunks.

1 Heat the oil in a wok. When the oil is just beginning to smoke, carefully add the beans and fry them for about 1–2 minutes until just tender.

2 Lift out the green beans on to a plate lined with kitchen paper. Using a ladle carefully remove all but 30ml/2 tbsp of oil from the wok.

3 Reheat the remaining oil, add the ginger and stir-fry for a minute or two to flavour the oil.

4 Return the green beans to the wok, stir in the agave syrup and soy sauce and season with salt and pepper. Toss together quickly to ensure the beans are well coated. Serve immediately.

Energy 108kcal/448kJ; Protein 1.5g; Carbohydrate 3.7g, of which sugars 2.2g; Fat 9.6g, of which saturates 1.2g; Cholesterol 0mg; Calcium 13mg; Fibre 2.5g; Sodium 3mg.
Energy 170kcal/698kJ; Protein 1.5g; Carbohydrate 3.2g, of which sugars 2.6g; Fat 16.9g, of which saturates 2.1g; Cholesterol 0mg; Calcium 28mg; Fibre 1.7g; Sodium 119mg.

desserts

The perfect way to round off a vegan dinner party is with a luxurious dessert that will really surprise your guests – especially non-vegan guests. Fruit desserts are always an excellent choice, with their naturally sweet flavours. Try Vanilla, Date and Saffron Pears, which are poached in agave syrup. There are also more indulgent treats in this chapter that many people believe vegans have to go without, such as Tofu Berry Cheesecake, Plum Charlottes with Calvados Cream and Baked Pumpkin with Coconut Custard. In addition, you will find you are spoilt for choice with the delectable ice creams and sorbets.

Date and tofu ice

Generously spiced with cinnamon and full of dried fruit, this delicious and unusual ice cream is also packed with plenty of soya protein. It also contains omega 3 fats and no added sugar.

Serves 4

250g/9oz/1½ cups stoned (pitted) dates
600ml/1 pint/2½ cups apple juice
5ml/1 tsp ground cinnamon
285g/10½oz pack chilled fresh tofu, cubed
150ml/¼ pint/⅔ cup unsweetened soya milk
60ml/4 tbsp hemp or flax oil
8 walnut halves, to decorate

1 Put the dates in a pan. Pour in 300ml/½ pint/1¼ cups of the apple juice and set aside to let the dates soak in the juice for 2 hours.

2 Bring the mixture to the boil and then simmer gently for 10 minutes. Set aside to cool then, using a slotted spoon, lift out about one-quarter of the dates. Chop them roughly and set aside.

3 Blend the remaining dates in a food processor or blender to a smooth purée. Add the cinnamon and process with enough of the remaining apple juice to make a smooth paste.

4 Add the tofu to the food processor, a few at a time, processing after each addition. Pour in the remaining apple juice and the soya milk and mix well.

5 Churn the mixture in an ice cream maker until very thick, but not thick enough to scoop. Scrape the ice cream into a plastic tub.

6 Stir in most of the chopped dates, retaining a few pieces for decorating, and freeze for 2–3 hours until firm.

7 Scoop into dessert glasses and decorate with the remaining chopped dates and the walnut halves.

Variation
You could make this tasty ice cream with any soft dried fruits; dried figs, apricots or peaches would be especially good. Alternatively, you could use a combination for a vitamin- and fibre-packed feast.

Energy 290kcal/1232kJ; Protein 9.1g; Carbohydrate 58.2g, of which sugars 57.9g; Fat 3.9g, of which saturates 0.5g; Cholesterol 0mg; Calcium 407mg; Fibre 2.5g; Sodium 24mg.

Coconut sorbet

You may have already had a few sorbets in your time if you have been avoiding dairy. This tropical version from South-east Asia proves they do not have to be restricted to orange or lemon.

Serves 6

250ml/8fl oz/1 cup agave syrup
120ml/4fl oz/½ cup coconut milk
50g/2oz/⅔ cup grated or desiccated
   (dry unsweetened shredded) coconut
a squeeze of lime juice

1 Place the agave syrup in a heavy pan and add 200ml/7fl oz/scant 1 cup water. Bring to the boil, stirring the mixture constantly.

2 Stir the coconut milk into the syrup, along with most of the grated or desiccated coconut and the lime juice. Pour the mixture into a bowl or freezer container and freeze for 2 hours.

3 Take the sorbet out of the freezer and beat it with a fork, or blend it in a food processor, until smooth and creamy. Return it to the freezer for 30 minutes.

4 Remove the sorbet from the freezer again and beat it with a fork, or blend it in a food processor, until it is smooth and creamy. Then return it to the freezer and leave until completely frozen.

5 Before serving, allow the sorbet to stand at room temperature for about 10–15 minutes to allow it to soften slightly. Serve in small bowls and decorate with the remaining grated or desiccated coconut.

Cook's tip
If using fresh coconut, serve the sorbet in the shells.

Energy 170kcal/717kJ; Protein 0.7g; Carbohydrate 32g, of which sugars 32g; Fat 5.2g, of which saturates 4.5g; Cholesterol 0mg; Calcium 23mg; Fibre 1.2g; Sodium 26mg.

Oranges with caramel wigs

These attractive oranges make the perfect dessert to serve at a dinner party as you can prepare them beforehand. The slightly bitter, caramelized orange rind and syrup has a wonderful flavour and texture that sits in perfect contrast to the sweet, juicy oranges.

Serves 6

6 oranges
120g/4oz/generous ½ cup soft light
  brown sugar
120ml/4fl oz/½ cup boiling water
cocktail sticks (toothpicks)

1 Using a vegetable peeler, thinly pare the rind off a few of the oranges to make 12 long strips.

2 Using a sharp knife, peel all the oranges, reserving the rind and discarding the pith. Reserve the juice and freeze the oranges separately for 30 minutes.

3 Slice the oranges, reform and secure with cocktail sticks. Chill.

4 Put half the sugar into a pan and add 15ml/1 tbsp water. Heat gently until the mixture caramelizes, shaking the pan a little if one side starts to brown too fast.

5 As soon as the mixture colours, dip the bottom of the pan into cold water. Add 30ml/2 tbsp hot water and the orange rind to the caramel, then stir until the caramel dissolves. Turn the rind on to a plate, to cool.

6 Make a caramel syrup for serving. Put the remaining sugar in a small pan with 15ml/1 tbsp water, and make caramel as before. When it has coloured nicely, stand well back, pour in the boiling water and stir with a wooden spoon to dissolve. Add the reserved juices and pour into a serving jug (pitcher).

7 To serve, arrange the orange strips in a criss-cross pattern on top of each orange. Remove the cocktail sticks and pour a little caramel syrup round the base of each orange.

Energy 122kcal/521kJ; Protein 1.4g; Carbohydrate 30.8g, of which sugars 30.8g; Fat 0.1g, of which saturates 0g; Cholesterol 0mg; Calcium 66mg; Fibre 2g; Sodium 7mg.

Vanilla, date and saffron pears

These sweet juicy pears, poached in agave syrup infused with vanilla, saffron and lime, make a truly elegant dessert. For a low-fat version you can eat them on their own, but for a really luxurious, indulgent treat, serve with soya, cashew or coconut ice cream.

Serves 4

2 vanilla pods (beans)
250ml/8fl oz/1 cup agave syrup
5ml/1 tsp finely grated lime rind
a large pinch of saffron
475ml/16fl oz/2 cups apple juice
4 large, firm ripe dessert pears
vegan ice cream, to serve

1 Using a small sharp knife, carefully split the vanilla pods in half. Scrape the seeds into a heavy pan large enough to hold all the pears, then add the vanilla pods as well.

2 Pour the agave syrup into the pan with the vanilla, then add the lime rind and the saffron. Pour the apple juice into the pan and bring the mixture to the boil. Reduce the heat to low and simmer, stirring occasionally, while you prepare the pears.

3 Peel the pears, then add to the pan and gently turn in the syrup to coat evenly. Cover the pan and simmer gently for about 12–15 minutes, turning the pears halfway through cooking, until they are just tender.

4 Lift the pears from the syrup using a slotted spoon and transfer to four serving bowls. Set aside.

5 Bring the syrup back to the boil and cook gently for about 10 minutes, or until the liquid has reduced slightly and thickened. Spoon the syrup over the pears and serve either warm or chilled with ice cream.

Cook's tip
For the best results use firm varieties of dessert pears, such as comice or conference, that are well ripened.

Variation
Try using different flavourings in the syrup. Use 10ml/2 tsp chopped fresh root ginger and 1 or 2 star anise in place of the saffron and vanilla, or 1 cinnamon stick, 3 cloves and 105ml/7tbsp maple syrup in place of the agave syrup.

Energy 283kcal/1207kJ; Protein 0.8g; Carbohydrate 74.3g, of which sugars 74.3g; Fat 0.2g, of which saturates 0g; Cholesterol 0mg; Calcium 38mg; Fibre 3.3g; Sodium 10mg.

Baked figs with hazelnut and maple syrup tofu ice cream

Figs have been cultivated for thousands of years, and with their deliciously intense flavour it is easy to see why. The nutty tofu ice cream is the perfect complement to these ancient fruits.

Serves 4

1 lemon grass stalk, finely chopped
1 cinnamon stick, roughly broken
60ml/4 tbsp maple syrup
200ml/7fl oz/scant 1 cup apple juice
8 large or 12 small figs

For the hazelnut soya ice cream
450ml/¾ pint/scant 2 cups soya cream
30ml/2 tbsp soya margarine
50ml/2fl oz/¼ cup maple syrup
45ml/3 tbsp silken tofu
1.5ml/¼ tsp vanilla extract
75g/3oz/¾ cup hazelnuts

1 In a bowl, blend together the ice cream ingredients, except for the hazelnuts, using an electric or hand whisk.

2 Transfer the ice cream mixture to a metal or plastic freezer container and freeze for 2 hours, or until the mixture feels firm around the edge.

3 Preheat the oven to 180°C/350°F/Gas 4. Place the hazelnuts on a baking sheet and roast for 10–12 minutes, or until they are golden brown. Leave the nuts to cool, then place them in a food processor or blender and process until they are coarsely ground.

4 Remove the container from the freezer and whisk the ice cream to break down the ice crystals. Stir in the ground hazelnuts and freeze the mixture again until half-frozen. Whisk again, then freeze until firm.

Cook's tips
• If you prefer, rather than whisking the semi-frozen ice cream, transfer it into a food processor and process until smooth.
• There are several types of figs available and they can all be used in this recipe. Choose from the green-skinned figs that have an amber-coloured flesh, dark purple-skinned fruit with a deep red flesh or green/yellow-skinned figs with a pinky-coloured flesh.

Variation
This recipe also works well with halved, stoned (pitted) nectarines or peaches, baked in the same way.

5 Place the lemon grass, cinnamon stick, maple syrup and apple juice in a small pan and heat slowly until boiling. Lower the heat and simmer the mixture for 5 minutes, then leave the syrup to stand for 15 minutes.

6 Preheat the oven to 200°C/400°F/Gas 6. Meanwhile, carefully cut the figs into quarters, leaving them intact at the bases. Place the figs in an ovenproof baking dish and pour over the maple-flavoured syrup.

7 Cover the dish tightly with foil and bake the figs for about 15 minutes, or until they are tender.

8 Take the ice cream from the freezer about 10 minutes before serving, to allow it to soften slightly. While still warm, transfer the baked figs to individual serving plates.

9 Drizzle a little of the spiced syrup over the figs. Serve them with a scoop or two of hazelnut ice cream.

Energy 500kcal/2098kJ; Protein 12.5g; Carbohydrate 62.8g, of which sugars 62.4g; Fat 23.2g, of which saturates 4.3g; Cholesterol 1mg; Calcium 280mg; Fibre 5.9g; Sodium 248mg.

Raw Key lime pie

The classic lime dessert originated in the Florida Keys and is now an American favourite. Here it enjoys a raw healthy makeover for vegans with the usual eggs and condensed milk replaced with a mix of avocado and coconut to give a creamy dessert that is packed with vitamin E.

Serves 6

For the filling
75g/3oz/6 tbsp extra virgin cold-pressed coconut oil
250g/9oz avocado flesh, roughly 2 medium avocados with skin and stones (pits) removed
75g/3oz/scant ½ cup ready-to-eat dried apricots
10ml/2 tsp pumpkin seed oil
finely grated rind of 2 limes
juice of 1 lime
15ml/1 tbsp agave syrup

For the base
50g/2oz/½ cup ground pumpkin seeds
50g/2oz/½ cup ground almonds
75g/3oz/½ cup medjool dates, chopped
15ml/1 tbsp agave syrup

1 Blend together all the ingredients for the base in a food processor or blender until you have a nice firm dough.

2 Lightly oil a 20cm/8in pie dish. Scrape the dough from the processor or blender and press the dough into the base of the dish, ensuring it is evenly distributed.

3 Melt the coconut oil in a heatproof bowl resting in a pan of hot water.

4 Blend together the avocados, dried apricots, pumpkin oil, and lime rind and juice in a food processor or blender. Gradually stir in the melted coconut oil.

5 Spread the mixture evenly on to the pie base using a palette knife or metal spatula. Chill for about 2 hours.

6 Serve decorated with thinly sliced lime twists, if you like.

Energy 360kcal/1494kJ; Protein 4.9g; Carbohydrate 15.4g, of which sugars 13.1g; Fat 31.4g, of which saturates 12.4g; Cholesterol 0mg; Calcium 48mg; Fibre 3.6g; Sodium 20mg.

Tofu berry cheesecake

This is a relatively low-sugar dessert, considering how delightful it tastes. Natural sugars in the fruit and apple juice sweeten the cheesecake, while the low-fat tofu and soya yogurt make it deliciously creamy – a perfect foil to the delicious summer fruits.

Serves 6

425g/15oz firm tofu
300g/11oz/scant 2 cups soya yogurt
1 sachet powdered vegetarian jelly crystals
90ml/6 tbsp apple juice
175g/6oz soft fruits, such as raspberries,
   strawberries and blueberries
30ml/2 tbsp redcurrant jelly
30ml/2 tbsp lemon juice, heated

For the base
50g/2oz/¼ cup dairy-free spread or
   soya margarine
30ml/2 tbsp apple juice
115g/4oz/6 cups bran flakes

1 To make the base, place the dairy-free spread or soya margarine and apple juice in a pan and heat them gently until the spread or margarine has melted. Crush the cereal and stir it into the apple juice mixture.

2 Transfer the mixture into a 23cm/9in loose-based round flan tin (pan) and press down firmly with your fingers. Leave the base to cool. Chill until set.

3 To make the filling, place the tofu and yogurt in a food processor and process them until smooth. Heat the apple juice, then add the jelly crystals until dissolved, and blend into the tofu mixture.

4 Spread the tofu mixture over the base, smoothing it evenly. Chill for 1–2 hours, until the filling has set.

5 Carefully remove the flan tin and place the cheesecake on a serving plate.

6 Arrange the fruits on top of the cake. Place the redcurrant jelly in a small bowl and add the heated lemon juice.

7 Stir the mixture well until the jelly has completely melted. Leave it to cool slightly and then spoon or lightly brush it over the fruit. Chill until required and then serve.

Health benefit
Made from soya beans, tofu is an excellent source of protein and it is low in fat, making this dessert a well-balanced dish. It is packed with vitamins and health-giving nutrients in the fruit and fibre in the bran-flake base.

Energy 175kcal/735kJ; Protein 8.1g; Carbohydrate 23.2g, of which sugars 13.7g; Fat 6g, of which saturates 1.4g; Cholesterol 1mg; Calcium 314mg; Fibre 2.8g; Sodium 241mg.

Pumpkin with vodka and cinnamon syrup

This unusual dish is based on a traditional dessert from the Far East. Pumpkin wedges are baked in the oven with brown sugar and plenty of vodka, which results in a delicious syrup.

Serves 6

1 small pumpkin, about 800g/1¾lb
350g/12oz/1½ cups soft dark brown sugar
120ml/4fl oz/½ cup vodka
5ml/1 tsp ground cloves
12 cinnamon sticks, each about 10cm/4in
    in length
fresh mint sprigs, to decorate
soya yogurt, to serve

1 Preheat the oven to 190ºC/375ºF/ Gas 5. Halve the pumpkin, remove the seeds and fibres and cut into wedges. Arrange in a shallow, flameproof casserole or heavy ovenproof dish. Fill the hollows with the sugar.

2 Pour the vodka carefully into the pan, taking care not to wash all the sugar to the bottom. Make sure that some of the vodka trickles down to the bottom to prevent the pumpkin from burning. Sprinkle on the ground cloves and add two of the cinnamon sticks.

3 Cover the pan tightly and bake in the oven for about 30 minutes, or until the pumpkin is tender. Check the casserole or pan occasionally to make sure that the pumpkin does not dry out or catch on the bottom.

4 Transfer the pumpkin to a platter and pour the hot syrup over. Decorate each portion with mint and cinnamon sticks and serve with soya yogurt.

Variation
Try using sweet potato or papaya, in place of the pumpkin, if you like.

Energy 247kcal/1054kJ; Protein 1.2g; Carbohydrate 63.9g, of which sugars 63.2g; Fat 0.3g, of which saturates 0.1g; Cholesterol 0mg; Calcium 70mg; Fibre 1.3g; Sodium 4mg.

Caramelized pineapple with lemon grass

This stunning dessert, garnished with jewel-like pomegranate seeds, is superb for entertaining. The tangy, zesty flavours of lemon grass and mint bring out the exquisite sweetness of the fruit.

Serves 4

30ml/2 tbsp very finely chopped lemon grass, and 2 lemon grass stalks, halved lengthways
450ml/¾ pint/scant 2 cups agave syrup
10ml/2 tsp chopped fresh mint leaves
150ml/¼ pint/⅔ cup pineapple juice
2 small, ripe pineapples
15ml/1 tbsp sunflower oil
60ml/4 tbsp pomegranate seeds
coconut cream, to serve

1 Place the chopped lemon grass, lemon grass stalks, 300ml/½ pint/1¼ cups of the agave syrup and the chopped mint leaves in a non-stick wok or large pan. Pour over the pineapple juice and bring to the boil over medium heat.

2 Reduce the heat and simmer the mixture for about 10–15 minutes, until thickened and reduced. Leave to cool slightly, then strain into a glass bowl, reserving the halved lemon grass stalks, then set aside.

3 Using a sharp knife, peel and core the pineapples and cut into 1cm/½in slices, then sprinkle the slices with the remaining agave syrup.

4 Brush a large non-stick wok or pan with the oil and place over a medium heat. Working in batches, cook the pineapple slices for 2–3 minutes on one side until they are just beginning to turn brown. Turn the slices over and cook the other side for another 2–3 minutes.

5 Transfer the pineapple slices to a flat serving dish and sprinkle over the pomegranate seeds.

6 Pour the lemon grass syrup over the fruit and garnish with the reserved stalks. Serve hot or at room temperature with coconut cream.

Cook's tip
To remove pomegranate seeds, halve the fruit and hold it over a bowl, cut side down. Tap all over with a wooden spoon or turn it completely inside out.

Energy 493kcal/2101kJ; Protein 1.7g; Carbohydrate 121.8g, of which sugars 121.8g; Fat 3.4g, of which saturates 0.3g; Cholesterol 0mg; Calcium 101mg; Fibre 3.6g; Sodium 11mg.

Plum charlottes with Calvados cream

There is a wide variety of plums and they can be used for much more than making into jam or turning into prunes. For this dish try seeking out and experimenting with the many different types – from tangy yellow greengages to sweet and juicy Victorias.

Serves 4

115g/4oz/½ cup soya margarine, melted
30ml/2 tbsp demerara (raw) sugar
450g/1lb ripe plums, stoned (pitted)
 and thickly sliced
50ml/2fl oz/¼ cup agave syrup
30ml/2 tbsp orange juice
1.5ml/¼ tsp ground cinnamon
25g/1oz/¼ cup ground almonds
8–10 large slices of wholemeal
 (whole-wheat) bread

For the Calvados sauce
5ml/1 tsp silken tofu
60ml/4 tbsp maple syrup
30ml/2 tbsp Calvados

1 Preheat the oven to 190°C/375°F/ Gas 5. Line the bases of four individual 10cm-/4in-diameter, deep, earthenware ramekin dishes with baking parchment. Brush evenly and thoroughly with a little of the melted soya margarine, then sprinkle each dish with a little of the demerara sugar, rotating the dish in your hands to make sure you coat each dish evenly.

Variations
• Slices of peeled pear or eating apples can be used in this recipe instead of the stoned, sliced plums.
• If you cannot find organic Calvados any organic fruit-based spirit will work in this dish.

2 Place the stoned plum slices in a pan with the agave syrup, orange juice and ground cinnamon and cook gently for 5 minutes, or until the plums have softened slightly. Leave the plums to cool, then stir in the ground almonds.

3 Cut the crusts off the bread and then use a plain pastry cutter to cut out four rounds to fit the bases of the ramekins. Dip the bread rounds into melted margarine and fit them into the dishes. Cut four more rounds to fit the tops of the dishes and set aside.

4 Cut the remaining bread into strips, dip into the melted margarine and use to line the sides of the ramekins.

5 Divide the plum mixture among the lined ramekins and level the tops. Place the bread rounds on top and brush with margarine. Place the ramekins on a baking sheet and bake for 25 minutes.

6 Make the sauce just before the charlottes are ready. Place the tofu and maple syrup in a large bowl, and blend them together until pale. Whisk in the Calvados. Continue whisking until the mixture is very light and frothy.

7 Remove the charlottes from the oven and turn out on to warm serving plates. Pour a little sauce over and around the charlottes and serve immediately.

Energy 600kcal/2513kJ; Protein 9.1g; Carbohydrate 69.6g, of which sugars 44.2g; Fat 32.5g, of which saturates 16.5g; Cholesterol 218mg; Calcium 128mg; Fibre 3.1g; Sodium 467mg.

Rice pudding with almonds

Rice is a popular dessert in many parts of the world. This delicious and healthy version of rice pudding is light and easy to make. The raisins benefit from pre-soaking in dry sherry before being added to the pudding. Top with orange segments or another tangy fruit of your choice.

Serves 4

75g/3oz/generous ½ cup raisins
75ml/5 tbsp dry sherry
90g/3½oz/½ cup short grain (pudding) rice
3 or 4 strips of pared lemon rind
250ml/8fl oz/1 cup rice milk
475ml/16fl oz/2 cups soya milk
1 cinnamon stick, about 7.5cm/3in in length,
   plus 3 more, to decorate
120ml/4fl oz/½ cup agave syrup
pinch of salt
5ml/1 tsp ground almonds
15g/½ oz/1 tbsp soya margarine
toasted flaked (sliced) almonds, to decorate
chilled orange segments, to serve

Cook's tip
Try drizzling with agave or maple syrup and sprinkle with nutmeg.

1 Put the raisins and dry sherry in a small pan. Heat gently until warm, then set the pan aside, which will allow the raisins to swell.

2 Mix the rice, lemon rind and rice milk in a heavy pan and bring the mixture gently to the boil. Lower the heat, cover the pan and simmer for approximately 20 minutes. Remove the lemon rind pieces from the pan with a slotted spoon and discard.

3 Add the soya milk and the cinnamon stick to the pan, then stir until the rice has absorbed the milk. Stir in the syrup and salt. Add the ground almonds and soya margarine. Stir until blended.

4 Drain the raisins and stir into the rice mixture. Cook for 2–3 minutes until heated through. Serve in individual bowls, topped with the toasted flaked almonds and orange segments, and decorate with a cinnamon stick.

Energy 325kcal/1365kJ; Protein 6.7g; Carbohydrate 56.2g, of which sugars 38.2g; Fat 6.3g, of which saturates 1.9g; Cholesterol 1mg; Calcium 44mg; Fibre 0.5g; Sodium 171mg.

Baked pumpkin with coconut custard

A vegan recipe based on a traditional dessert from Thailand. Once the custard-filled pumpkin is baked, the flesh is scooped out with the custard and a hot coconut sauce is drizzled over the top. Sweet and fragrant, this delicious dish is sheer indulgence and a real crowd pleaser.

Serves 4–6

1 small pumpkin, about 1.3kg/3lb, halved, seeded and fibres removed
400ml/14fl oz/1⅔ cups coconut milk
45ml/3 tbsp silken tofu
45ml/3 tbsp agave syrup, plus a little extra for drizzling
salt

For the sauce
250ml/8fl oz/1 cup coconut cream
30ml/2 tbsp agave syrup

1 Preheat the oven to 180°C/350°F/ Gas 4. Place the pumpkin halves, skin side down, in a baking dish.

2 In a large bowl, blend the coconut milk with a pinch of salt, the tofu and agave syrup, until the mixture is thick and smooth.

3 Pour the custard into each pumpkin half. Sprinkle a little extra agave syrup over the top of the custard and the rim of the pumpkin.

> **Variation**
> This recipe can also be made with butternut or acorn squash and, interestingly, with halved avocados, mangoes and papayas. Bear in mind that the quantity of custard and the cooking times may have to be adjusted.

4 Bake in the oven for 35–40 minutes. The pumpkin should feel tender when a skewer is inserted in it, and the custard should feel firm when lightly touched.
If you like, you can brown the top further under the grill (broiler).

5 Just before serving, heat the coconut cream in a pan with a pinch of salt and the syrup. Scoop out pieces of pumpkin flesh with the custard and place in bowls. Pour a little sweetened coconut cream over the top to serve.

Energy 217kcal/906kJ; Protein 4.5g; Carbohydrate 16.3g, of which sugars 15.7g; Fat 15.4g, of which saturates 11.9g; Cholesterol 71mg; Calcium 71mg; Fibre 1.3g; Sodium 88mg.

Chocolate and orange gateau

This indulgent cake is proof that vegans need not miss out on the luscious treats enjoyed by those who eat dairy products. Enjoy the look on diners' faces when you reveal it is a vegan cake.

Serves 8

250g/9oz/2¼ cups self-raising (self-rising) wholemeal (whole-wheat) flour
225g/8oz/1 cup soft light brown sugar
30ml/2 tbsp of unsweetened cocoa powder
10ml/2 tsp carob powder
120ml/4fl oz/½ cup rapeseed (canola) oil
150ml/¼ pint/⅔ cup soya milk
115g/4oz/1 cup broken walnuts
rind of 2 oranges
15ml/1 tbsp vegan yogurt or tofu
15ml/1 tbsp balsamic vinegar
salt

For the filling
60ml/4 tbsp vegan cream cheese
5ml/1 tsp finely grated lime rind
60ml/4 tbsp marmalade or apricot jam

For the chocolate sauce
115g/4oz dairy-free dark (bittersweet) chocolate
15ml/1 tbsp agave syrup
15ml/1 tbsp orange liqueur (optional)
250ml/8fl oz/1 cup soya cream

1 Place all the ingredients for the cake mixture in a large bowl. Mix thoroughly with a wooden spoon until they are thoroughly combined.

2 Coarsely grate or chop up 25g/1oz of the dairy-free chocolate from the chocolate sauce ingredients. Stir it into the cake mixture.

3 Preheat the oven to 180°C/350°F/Gas 4. Lightly oil two 20cm/8in deep cake tins (pans) and line the bases with baking parchment. Spoon in the cake mixture evenly between the two tins.

4 Bake the cakes in the oven for about 20–30 minutes or until a metal skewer inserted in the centre comes out clean.

5 Meanwhile, prepare the filling. Put the cream cheese into a bowl and mix in the grated lime rind. Set aside until ready to use.

6 When the cakes are baked turn them out on to a wire rack. Leave them to cool completely.

7 When the cakes are cool, spread the lime cream cheese evenly over the top of one of the cakes. Spread the other with marmalade or jam. Sandwich them together with the two fillings facing each other and place on a plate.

8 Make the chocolate sauce. Break the chocolate into chunks and melt in a bowl set over a pan of boiling water. Mix in the agave syrup, liqueur, if using, and then the soya cream a little at a time while continuously stirring. Pour over the cake.

9 Leave to cool slightly, then serve with extra sauce, if you like.

Energy 536kcal/2245kJ; Protein 8.1g; Carbohydrate 68.9g, of which sugars 43.6g; Fat 26.9g, of which saturates 5.2g; Cholesterol 1mg; Calcium 99mg; Fibre 2.1g; Sodium 62mg.

Figgy pudding

This dessert is a delicious treat for grown-ups that will be the perfect end to a vegan meal.
The fruits are soaked in brandy and orange juice overnight to make them extremely succulent.

Serves 4

225g/8oz/2 cups self-raising (self-rising)
  wholemeal (whole-wheat) flour
115g/4oz/½ cup coconut fat (chilled)
300ml/½ pint/1¼ cups soya milk

For the filling
175g/6oz/1 cup dried figs
115g/4oz/½ cup prunes
75g/3oz/generous ½ cup raisins
  or sultanas (golden raisins)
50g/2oz/¼ cup ready-to-eat dried apricots
50g/2oz/⅓ cup dates
25g/1oz chopped apple
150ml/¼ pint/⅔ cup brandy
60ml/4 tbsp fresh orange juice
15ml/1 tbsp agave syrup
1.5ml/¼ tsp ground ginger
1.5ml/¼ tsp ground cinnamon

1 The night before making the pudding, place the dried figs, prunes, raisins or sultanas, apricots, dates and apple in a large bowl. Pour in the brandy and the orange juice and set aside to soak.

2 Next day remove any pits from the soaked dates and prunes. Sift the flour into a large bowl. Grate in the coconut fat and mix together with your fingers. Gradually add the soya milk, mixing until a soft dough forms.

3 Turn out the dough on to a floured surface and lightly knead until smooth. Roll out two-thirds of the dough into a round and use to line a well-oiled 1.2 litre/2 pint heatproof bowl.

4 Add the agave syrup, ginger and cinnamon to the soaked fruits and brandy mixture. Mix well and spoon the fruits into the pastry-lined bowl.

5 Moisten the edges of the pastry with soya milk. Cover with a lid rolled from the remaining dough. Press the edges together to seal.

6 Cover securely with oiled baking parchment tied with string. Place the bowl in a pan of simmering water that comes about halfway up the bowl. Simmer in the pan for about 2 hours. Ensure that the water does not evaporate, topping it up from time to time with boiling water.

7 Carefully turn the pudding out on to a plate, and serve immediately with cashew nut cream, oat milk custard or vegan ice cream, if you like.

Cook's tip
You can finely chop the dried fruit for a less chunky filling.

Energy 773kcal/3238kJ; Protein 13.2g; Carbohydrate 92.2g, of which sugars 56.2g; Fat 32.6g, of which saturates 25g; Cholesterol 0mg; Calcium 171mg; Fibre 11.2g; Sodium 71mg.

Bakewell tart

This traditional sweet almond tart is always the first to go at vegan food festivals. It is often attributed to Mrs Greaves, landlady of a pub in the English Peak District town of Bakewell in 1820. References have, however, been found to similar tarts dating back to medieval times.

3 Spread a layer of raspberry jam in the base of the pastry case (pie shell).

4 In a bowl, mix together the flour, ground almonds, sugar, lemon rind and baking powder. Add the oil, soya milk and extracts and mix again.

5 Pour the mixture over the jammy pastry base. Sprinkle with flaked almonds on top. Bake for 35 minutes.

6 Serve the tart warm with hot oat milk custard or soya ice cream.

Serves 8

60ml/4 tbsp raspberry jam
225g/8oz/2 cups wholemeal
  (whole-wheat) flour
50g/2oz/½ cup ground almonds
175g/6oz/¾ cup soft light brown sugar
5ml/1 tsp finely grated lemon rind
10ml/2 tsp baking powder
150ml/¼ pint/⅔ cup vegetable oil
200ml/7fl oz/scant 1 cup soya milk
5ml/1 tsp vanilla extract
5ml/1 tsp almond extract
25g/1oz flaked (sliced) almonds

For the pastry

250g/9oz/2¼ cups wholemeal
  (whole-wheat) flour
75ml/2½fl oz/⅓ cup rapeseed
  (canola) oil
15ml/1 tbsp sesame tahini
75ml/2½fl oz/⅓ cup sweetened soya milk

1 Preheat the oven to 190°C/375°F/Gas 5. Make the pastry. Rub together the flour, oil and tahini until it resembles breadcrumbs. Gradually add the soya milk and mix to form a soft dough.

2 Roll out the dough on a floured surface into a circle that will line a 20cm/8in oiled pie dish. Prick the dough all over with a fork and bake it in the oven for about 10–15 minutes. Set aside to cool.

Energy 538kcal/2257kJ; Protein 11g; Carbohydrate 66.9g, of which sugars 30g; Fat 26.9g, of which saturates 2.8g; Cholesterol 0mg; Calcium 76mg; Fibre 6.2g; Sodium 17mg.

Pumpkin pie

The colonists who settled in North America in the 17th century saw the Native Americans growing and eating pumpkins and they soon embraced this new food. This version of the classic dessert will be an essential part of any American Thanksgiving vegan feast.

Serves 6–8

350g/12oz silken tofu
450g/1lb stewed mashed pumpkin
7.5ml/1½ tsp ground cinnamon
2.5ml/½ tsp ground ginger
2.5ml/½ tsp ground nutmeg
5ml/1 tsp sea salt
5ml/1 tsp vanilla extract
15ml/1 tbsp carob molasses or agave syrup
260g/9½oz/generous 1 cup soft light
   brown sugar
75ml/2½fl oz/⅓ cup rapeseed (canola) oil

For the pastry
250g/9oz/2¼ cups wholemeal
   (whole-wheat) flour
7.5ml/1½ tsp ground cinnamon
75ml/2½fl oz/⅓ cup pumpkin seed oil
   or rapeseed (canola) oil
15ml/1 tbsp pumpkin seed or peanut butter
75ml/2½fl oz/⅓ cup sweetened soya milk

1 Make the pastry. Rub together the flour, cinnamon, oil and butter until it resembles breadcrumbs. Add soya milk to form a soft dough.

2 Roll out dough and line an oiled 20cm/8in pie dish. Preheat the oven to 180°C/350°F/Gas 4.

3 Mix all the ingredients for the filling in a food processor or blender until smooth and creamy.

4 Pour the filling into the unbaked pastry case (pie shell), and bake in the oven for 50 minutes to 1 hour until golden brown.

5 Carefully transfer the pie on to a plate. Chill in the refrigerator before serving.

Energy 434kcal/1809kJ; Protein 6.2g; Carbohydrate 35.3g, of which sugars 19.4g; Fat 30.8g, of which saturates 13.8g; Cholesterol 94mg; Calcium 108mg; Fibre 1.2g; Sodium 60mg.

Crunchy pear and apricot flan

Do not be tempted to add any sugar with the fruit, as this will cause them to produce too much liquid. All the sweetness that you will need is in the pastry and the delicious crunchy topping.

Serves 8

75g/3oz/6 tbsp soya margarine
175g/6oz/1½ cups wholemeal
   (whole-wheat) flour
25g/1oz/¼ cup ground almonds
15ml/1 tbsp soya milk
30ml/2 tbsp agave syrup
1.5ml/¼ tsp almond extract
sifted icing (confectioners') sugar, for dusting

For the crunchy topping
115g/4oz/1 cup wholemeal
   (whole-wheat) flour
1.5ml/¼ tsp mixed (pumpkin pie) spice
50g/2oz/¼ cup soya margarine
60ml/4 tbsp agave syrup
50g/2oz/½ cup flaked (sliced) almonds

For the filling
450g/1lb pears
30ml/2 tbsp raisins or sultanas (golden raisins)
225g/8oz ready-to-eat dried apricots, chopped

1 To make the pastry, rub the soya margarine into the flour, either with your fingertips in a large mixing bowl or in a food processor, until the mixture resembles fine breadcrumbs.

2 Mix the soya milk with the agave syrup and almond extract and stir into the dry ingredients to form a soft, pliable dough. Knead the dough lightly on a floured surface until smooth, wrap in clear film (plastic wrap) and set aside until ready to roll out.

3 Meanwhile, make the crunchy topping. Sift the flour and mixed spice into a bowl and rub in the margarine. Stir in the agave syrup and almonds.

4 Roll out the dough on a lightly floured surface and use it to line a 23cm/9in loose-based flan tin (pan), taking care to press it neatly into the edges and to make a lip around the top edge.

5 Roll off the excess pastry to neaten the edge. Leave to chill in the refrigerator for about 15 minutes.

6 Preheat the oven to 190°C/375°F/ Gas 5. Place a baking sheet in the oven to preheat. Peel, core and slice the pears thinly. Arrange the slices on top of the pastry in overlapping, concentric circles, doming the centre. Sprinkle over the raisins or sultanas and apricots. The flan will seem too full at this stage, but the pears will reduce down during cooking and the filling will drop slightly.

7 Cover the apples with the crunchy topping mixture, pressing it down lightly. Bake on the hot baking sheet for 25–30 minutes, or until the top is golden brown. Test to make sure the pears are tender by inserting a metal skewer into them.

8 Leave the flan to cool in the tin for 10 minutes before turning out. Dust the top of the flan with icing sugar. The flan can be served either warm or cool.

Energy 397kcal/1664kJ; Protein 8.1g; Carbohydrate 51.4g, of which sugars 28.7g; Fat 19.1g, of which saturates 6.2g; Cholesterol 2mg; Calcium 69mg; Fibre 7g; Sodium 166mg.

Raspberry and almond tart

This is a beautifully rich tart, ideal for serving at the end of a special celebratory feast or at a dinner party. The raspberries and ground almonds are perfect partners.

Serves 4

200g/7oz sweet shortcrust pastry
125g/4¼oz silken tofu
75ml/2½fl oz/⅓ cup soya cream
50ml/2fl oz/¼ cup agave syrup
50g/2oz/½ cup ground almonds
20g/¾oz/1½ tbsp soya margarine
350g/12oz/2 cups raspberries

1 Roll out the sweet shortcrust pastry and use it to line a 20cm/8in flan tin (pan). Prick the base all over with a fork and leave it to rest for at least 30 minutes. Preheat the oven to 200°C/400°F/Gas 6.

2 Put the tofu, soya cream, agave syrup and ground almonds into a large bowl and whisk together briskly. Melt the margarine gently in a pan and pour into the mixture, stirring until the ingredients are well combined.

3 Sprinkle the raspberries over the pastry case (pie shell). The ones at the top will appear through the surface, so space them evenly or in a pattern.

4 Pour the tofu and almond mixture on top of the raspberries. Ensure that it is spread evenly over the tart and some fruits are poking out of the top.

5 Bake the tart in the preheated oven for 25 minutes. Leave to cool for 5 minutes. Serve warm or cold.

Variation

Peaches will also make a very attractive and tasty tart. Use six large, ripe peaches and remove the skin and stone (pit). Cut into slices and use in the same way as the raspberries above. You could also use mulberries if you can get them.

Energy 432kcal/1804kJ; Protein 10.4g; Carbohydrate 38.7g, of which sugars 15.3g; Fat 27.2g, of which saturates 7.8g; Cholesterol 19mg; Calcium 262mg; Fibre 4.1g; Sodium 297mg.

Apple and walnut strudel

This crisp pastry roll, filled with a delicious mix of fruit and jam, is the perfect sweet treat to accompany a cup of tea. No one can resist a slice of strudel served with a glass of lemon tea.

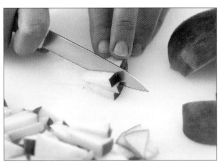

3 Preheat the oven to 180°C/350°F/ Gas 4. To make the filling, core and finely chop the apples but do not peel. Put the apples in a bowl, add the sultanas or raisins, syrup, walnuts, cinnamon and apricot jam or conserve and mix together until well combined.

4 Divide the pastry into three equal pieces. Place one piece on a sheet of lightly floured baking parchment and roll out to a rectangle measuring about 45 x 30cm/18 x 12in.

5 Spread one-third of the filling over the pastry, leaving a 1–2cm/½–¾in border. Roll up the pastry to enclose the filling and place, seam side down, on a non-stick baking sheet.

Makes 3, each serves 4–6

250g/9oz/generous 1 cup soya margarine
250g/9oz/generous 1 cup silken tofu
60ml/4 tbsp agave syrup
5ml/1 tsp vanilla extract
large pinch of salt
250g/9oz/2¼ cups wholemeal
   (whole-wheat) flour
icing (confectioners') sugar, sifted,
   for dusting

For the filling

2–3 cooking apples
45–60ml/3–4 tbsp sultanas
   (golden raisins) or raisins
45ml/3 tbsp agave syrup
115g/4oz/1 cup walnuts, roughly chopped
5–10ml/1–2 tsp ground cinnamon
60ml/4 tbsp apricot jam or conserve

1 To make the pastry, beat the margarine until light and fluffy, then add the tofu, agave syrup, vanilla extract and salt, and beat together.

2 Sift the flour into the mixture and stir until a soft dough forms. Wrap the dough in clear film (plastic wrap) and chill in the refrigerator overnight or until needed.

6 Repeat with the remaining pastry and filling. Bake the strudels for 25–30 minutes until golden brown all over.

7 Remove the strudels from the oven and leave to rest for 5 minutes to allow them to firm up slightly. Dust them liberally with icing sugar. Serve either warm or cold.

Energy 232kcal/967kJ; Protein 4g; Carbohydrate 17.7g, of which sugars 9g; Fat 16.6g, of which saturates 5.5g; Cholesterol 2mg; Calcium 87mg; Fibre 1.8g; Sodium 129mg.

Chocolate brownies

Dark and full of flavour, these brownies are irresistible. They are a perfect after-dinner treat or an ideal accompaniment to a cup of herbal tea. They also make a fabulous gift for a vegan friend.

Makes 20

150g/5oz/⅔ cup soya margarine
150g/5oz/scant 1 cup pitted dates,
    softened in boiling water,
    then drained and finely chopped
150g/5oz/1¼ cups self-raising (self-rising)
    wholemeal (whole-wheat) flour
10ml/2 tsp baking powder
60ml/4 tbsp unsweetened cocoa powder
    dissolved in 30ml/2 tbsp hot water
60ml/4 tbsp apple and pear fruit spread
90ml/6 tbsp soya milk
50g/2oz/½ cup pecan nuts, roughly broken

1 Preheat the oven to 160°C/325°F/ Gas 3. Lightly grease a shallow baking tin (pan), measuring approximately 28 x 18cm/11 x 7in.

2 Cream the soya margarine with the chopped dates in a large bowl until the mixture is well combined.

3 Sift the flour with the baking powder into the margarine and date mixture and mix thoroughly.

4 In a separate bowl, whisk together the dissolved cocoa powder with the apple and pear fruit spread.

5 Gradually pour the soya milk into the cocoa and spread mixture, whisking constantly to combine the ingredients. Pour into the flour mixture, stirring with a wooden spoon until everything is well mixed. Stir the pecan nuts into the bowl.

6 Spoon the mixture into the prepared tin, smooth the surface and bake for about 45–50 minutes or until a metal skewer inserted in the centre comes out clean.

7 Cool for a few minutes in the tin, then cut into bars or squares. Transfer to a wire rack and leave to cool.

Cook's tip
Apple and pear fruit spread is made from concentrated fruit juice. Look for the additive-free versions available in health-food stores and larger supermarkets.

Variation
You can use other nuts in the brownies if you prefer. Try using walnuts or hazelnuts, or a mixture.

Energy 135kcal/563kJ; Protein 2.2g; Carbohydrate 12.6g, of which sugars 7.5g; Fat 8.8g, of which saturates 3.3g; Cholesterol 1mg; Calcium 13mg; Fibre 1.5g; Sodium 91mg.

Societies and shopping

There are many vegan societies around the world. They provide information and advice on ways of living a life that is free from animal products. There are also plenty of stores selling a range of vegan products, from food and drink to clothing, shoes and toiletries.

United Kingdom

The Vegan Society,
Donald Watson House,
21 Hylton Street,
Hockley,
Birmingham
B18 6HJ
Tel: 0121 523 1730
www.vegansociety.com

Vegan Village
www.veganvillage.co.uk

Beyond Skin
34 Westbourne Gardens
Hove, East Sussex
BN3 5PP
Tel: 0845 373 3648
www.beyondskin.co.uk

Bourgeois Boheme
Hydrex House,
Garden Road
Richmond
TW9 4NR
Tel: 0208 878 8388
www.bboheme.com

Essential Trading Co-operative Ltd
Unit 3
Lodge Causeway Trading Estate
Fishponds, Bristol
BS16 3JB
Tel: 0117 958 3550
www.essential-trading.co.uk

Ethical Junction CIC
112 Lyndhurst Road
Ashurst, Southampton
Hampshire
SO40 7AU
Tel: 023 8029 3763
www.ethical-junction.org/directory

Foods for Life Nutritionists
96-98 High Street,
Croydon
CR0 1ND
Tel: 0871 288 4642
www.optimumnutritionists.com

GoodnessDirect
South March, Daventry
NN11 4PH
Tel: 0871 871 6611
www.GoodnessDirect.co.uk

The Health Store
Unit 10, Blenheim Park Road
Nottingham
NG6 8YP
Tel: 0115 976 7200
www.thehealthstore.co.uk

Highland Wholefoods Workers
Cooperative Ltd
Unit 6, 13 Harbour Road
Inverness
IV1 1SY
Tel: 01463 712393
www.highlandwholefoods.co.uk

Holland and Barrett
Samuel Ryder House, Townsend Drive
Nuneaton
CV11 6XW
Tel: 0870 606 6605
www.hollandandbarrett.com

Lush Cosmetics
Unit 3, 19 Willis Way,
Fleets Industrial Estate,
Poole,
BH15 3SS
Tel: 01202 668545
www.lush.co.uk

National Association of Health Stores
PO Box 14177,
Tranent,
EH34 5WX
Tel: 01875-341 408
www.nahs.co.uk

Plamil Foods Ltd
Folkestone
Kent
CT19 6PQ
Tel: 01303 850588
www.plamilfoods.co.uk

The Redwood Wholefood Co. Ltd
Redwood House, Burkitt Road
Earlstrees Industrial Estate,
Corby
NN17 4DT
Tel: 01536 400557
www.redwoodfoods.co.uk

Suma Wholefoods
Lacy Way,
Lowfields Business Park,
Elland
HX5 9DB
Tel: 01422 313845
www.suma.co.uk

Traidcraft Plc
Kingsway
Gateshead
Tyne and Wear
NE11 0NE
Tel: 0845 330 8900
www.traidcraftshop.co.uk

Vegan Store Ltd
PO Box 110
Rottingdean
Brighton
BN51 9AZ
www.veganstore.co.uk

Yaoh
PO Box 333
Bristol
BS99 1NF
Tel: 0117 9239053
www.yaoh.co.uk

USA

American Vegan Society
56 Dinshah Lane
P.O. Box 369
Malaga NJ 08328
Tel: (856) 694-2887
www.americanvegan.org

Earth Save
http://www.earthsave.org/

Alternative Outfitters
Suite 1, 408 S. Pasadena Ave
Pasadena, CA 91105
Tel: (626) 396-4972
www.alternativeoutfitters.com

Different Daisy
515 Second Street
Portsmouth OH 45662
Tel: (740) 935-3146
www.differentdaisy.com

Flora Inc.
Post Office Box 73
805 E. Badger Road
Lynden
Washington 98264
Tel: 1-800-446-2110
www.florahealth.com

Green People
Suite #206
41 Highland Ave
Highland Park NJ 08904
Tel: (732) 514-1066
www.greenpeople.org

The Hain Celestial Group 4600
Sleepytime Dr.
Boulder, CO 80301
Tel: 1-800-434-4246
www.hain-celestial.com

Organic Consumers Association
6771 South Silver Hill Drive
Finland MN 55603
Tel: (218) 226-4164
www.organicconsumers.org

Whole Foods Market, Inc.
550 Bowie Street
Austin TX 78703-4644
Tel: (512) 477-4455
www.wholefoodsmarket.com

Vegan Store
2381 Lewis Ave
Rockville MD 20851
1-800-340-1200
www.veganstore.com

Vegan essentials
Unit 8, 1701 Pearl St
Waukesha WI 53186
Tel: (262) 574-7761
www.veganessentials.com

Australia

The Vegan Society of Australia
PO Box 85
Seaford
VIC 3198
Tel: (03) 9776 4425
www.veganaustralia.net

Vegetarian/Vegan Society
of Queensland
1086 Waterworks Road
The Gap QLD 4061
Tel: (07) 3300 9320
www.vegsoc.org.au

Vegan Society NSW
PO Box 467
Broadway NSW 2007
Tel: (02) 9544 3328
www.vegansocietynsw.com

The Cruelty Free Shop
76 Waratah St
Haberfield NSW 2045
Tel: (02) 9799 4776
www.crueltyfreeshop.com.au

Fundamental food store
140 Keen Street
Lismore NSW 2480
Tel: (02) 6622 2199
www.fundies.com.au

Only Australian Groceries
1/ 37 Queens Rd, Everton Hills
Brisbane QLD 4053
Tel: (07) 3353 5782
www.onlyoz.com.au

Vegan Perfection
59 Queen St
Altona VIC 3018
Tel: (03) 9398 6302
www.veganperfection.com.au

Vegan Wares (shoes)
78 Smith Street
Collingwood 3066
Tel: (03) 9417 0230
www.veganwares.com

New Zealand

Porphyry's People
www.vegan.org.nz

Green Peace
Private Bag 92507
Wellesley Street, Auckland 1141
Tel: (09) 630 6317
www.gefreefood.org.nz/outlets.asp

Sanitarium Health Food Company
Private Bag 92127
Auckland 1142
Tel: 0800 100 257
www.sanitarium.co.nz

Wrights Vegan Wines
Tel: (06) 868 0967
www.wrightswines.co.nz

World Vegan Day

www.wvd.org.au
www.worldveganday.org.uk
www.vegansworldnetwork.org

Index

Acknowledgements

Picture acknowledgements:
iStockphoto p6t & 8b.

Photographers: Karl Adamson; Edward Allwright; Peter Anderson; Caroline Arber; David Armstrong; Tim Auty; Steve Baxter; Martin Brigdale; Louisa Dare; Nicki Dowey; Micki Dowie; James Duncan; Gus Filgate; John Freeman; Ian Garlick; Michelle Garrett; Will Heap; Peter Henley; John Heseltine; Amanda Heywood; Ferguson Hill; Janine Hosegood; Becky Johnson; David Jordan; Maris Kelly; Dave King; Don Last; William Lingwood; Patrick McLeavey; Michael Michaels; Steve Moss; Roisin Neild; Thomas Odulate; Spike Powell; Craig Robertson; Bridget Sargeson; Simon Smith; Sam Stowell; Polly Wreford.

Recipe writers: Pepita Aris; Catherine Atkinson; Josephine Bacon; Mridula Baljekar; Jane Bamforth; Mary Banks; Alex Barker; Valerie Barrett; Ghillie Başan; Judy Bastyra; Steve Baxter; Michelle Berridale-Johnson; Susannah Blake; Angela Boggiano; Janet Brinkworth; Kathy Brown; Carla Capalbo; Kit Chan; Jacqueline Clark; Maxine Clark; Carole Clements; Andi Clevely; Trish Davies; Roz Denny; Patrizia Diemling; Matthew Drennan; Tessa Evelegh; Joanna Farrow; Rafi Fernandez; Marina Filippelli; Jenni Fleetwood; Christine France; Silvana Franco; Yasuko Fukuoka; Sarah Gates; Shirley Gill; Brian Glover; Nicola Graimes; Rosamund Grant; Carole Handslip; Juliet Harbutt; Rebekah Hassan; Shehzad Husain;

Deh-Ta Hsuing; Christine Ingram; Judy Jackson; Becky Johnson; Bridget Jones; Peter Jordan; Manisha Kanani; Soheila Kimberley; Lucy Knox; Masaki Ko; Elisabeth Lambert Ortiz; Ruby Le Bois; Clare Lewis; Sara Lewis; Lesley Mackley; Norma MacMillan; Sue Maggs; Kathy Man; Sally Mansfield; Elizabeth Martin; Maggie Mayhew; Christine McFadden; Norma Miller; Jane Milton; Sallie Morris; Annie Nichols; Suzannah Olivier; Maggie Pannell; Katherine Richmond; Keith Richmond; Rena Salaman; Jennie Shapter; Anne Sheasby; Ysanne Spevack; Marlene Spieler; Jenny Stacey; Liz Trigg; Christopher Trotter; Linda Tubby; Oona van den Berg; Sunil Vijayaker; Hilaire Walden; Laura Washburn; Steven

Wheeler; Jenny White; Kate Whiteman; Lucy Whiteman; Rosemary Wilkinson; Carol Wilson; Elizabeth Wolf-Cohen; Jeni Wright.

Food stylists and home economists: Eliza Baird; Alex Barker; Caroline Barty; Angela Boggiano; Fergal Connolly; Joanne Craig; Nicki Dowey; Tonia George; Joanna Farrow; Christine France; Silvana Franco; Annabel Ford; Carole Handslip; Jo Harris; Amanda Heywood; Claire Louise Hunt; Kate Jay; Becky Johnson; Jill Jones; Emma MacIntosh; Penny Markham; Lucy McKelvie; Sarah O'Brien; Marion Price; Bridget Sargeson; Jennie Shapter; Carol Tennant; Helen Trent; Linda Tubby; Sunil Vijayaker; Jenny White; Elizabeth Wolf-Cohen.